truth heals

truth heals

WHAT YOU HIDE CAN HURT YOU

DEBORAH KING

HAY HOUSE

Australia • Canada • Hong Kong • India
South Africa • United Kingdom • United States

First published and distributed in the United Kingdom by:
Hay House UK Ltd, 292B Kensal Rd, London W10 5BE. Tel.: (44) 20 8962 1230; Fax: (44) 20 8962 1239. www.hayhouse.co.uk

Published and distributed in the United States of America by:
Hay House, Inc., PO Box 5100, Carlsbad, CA 92018-5100. Tel.: (1) 760 431 7695 or (800) 654 5126; Fax: (1) 760 431 6948 or (800) 650 5115. www.hayhouse.com

Published and distributed in Australia by:
Hay House Australia Ltd, 18/36 Ralph St, Alexandria NSW 2015. Tel.: (61) 2 9669 4299; Fax: (61) 2 9669 4144. www.hayhouse.com.au

Published and distributed in the Republic of South Africa by:
Hay House SA (Pty), Ltd, PO Box 990, Witkoppen 2068. Tel./Fax: (27) 11 467 8904. www.hayhouse.co.za

Published and distributed in India by:
Hay House Publishers India, Muskaan Complex, Plot No.3, B-2, Vasant Kunj, New Delhi – 110 070. Tel.: (91) 11 4176 1620; Fax: (91) 11 4176 1630. www.hayhouse.co.in

Distributed in Canada by:
Raincoast, 9050 Shaughnessy St, Vancouver, BC V6P 6E5. Tel.: (1) 604 323 7100; Fax: (1) 604 323 2600

Visit our website at **www.truthheals.com** for more information.

A catalogue record for this book is available from the British Library.

ISBN 978-1-8485-0076-1

Printed in the UK by CPI William Clowes Beccles NR34 7TL

I would like to acknowledge all those who have sought my help over the years, in my private practice, at workshops, and at public events. Your belief that it is possible to live your lives fully—despite the past—and your faith in your own truth give this book its spirit.

ACKNOWLEDGMENTS

This project could not have been accomplished without the support, guidance, and influence of many people. Much gratitude goes to the following key individuals:

Parvati Markus, editor and friend, whose keen mind and literary wisdom are invaluable. More than an editor, she is also a contributor, researcher, and source of inspiration, not just for this book but for everything I write. My life has been blessed by her brilliance and friendship. Every day I am grateful for her sense of humor and insight into the creative process. With deep respect and enormous gratitude for our working partnership. Words cannot express my appreciation for all you have done and all that you are.

Louise Hay, Reid Tracy, and all the staff at Hay House: Stacey Smith, Margarete Nielsen, Heather Tate, Jeannie Liberati, Jacqui Clark, and Lindsay Condict, who were all instrumental in getting this message out; and Patricia Gift and Laura Koch, for their insights and literary polish, adding just the right touch.

A big thank you also goes to Marilyn Warren, organizational genius and long time friend, and Scott Hartley, marketing guru and tech guy extraordinaire, for keeping everything running smoothly and being so supportive.

Jan Stake for her accounting expertise and friendship.

Peter Hurley, L.Ac., for his professional review.

Chris Shull, for assisting with the initial draft and helping me turn my memoir and case histories into one cohesive whole; Maria Croke and Geralyn Gendreaux for their superb editing skills and enthusiasm for the many subsequent drafts.

Terri Jay, for her patient listening and enduring friendship.

Heather McElwain, Turtle Bay Design, for taking such professional pride in each and every step of the process.

Brand Navigation, whose artwork graces this cover and whose integrity and commitment to their work is a true inspiration.

Carl Studna, photographer extraordinaire, whose intimate portraits of such figures as Paul McCartney and the Dalai Lama are known worldwide.

But most of all, my work and this book would not be possible without my husband, Eric, who has always been by my side.

CONTENTS

Truth is like the sun.
You can shut it out for a time,
but it ain't goin' away.
— Elvis Presley

INTRODUCTION

A bumper sticker on a car in front of me reads:

In a world of deceit, telling the truth is a revolutionary act.

Truth heals. But how? And why? And what good does it do anyway?

Plenty.

Telling the truth is about freedom. It is about joy and peace and health and living a life that is meaningful, powerful, connected, and loving. Ultimately, telling the truth is about feeling good in your own skin, unencumbered, free, and having the life that you want to live.

So why do lies so often seem nicer, tidier, easier?

The truth is often uncomfortable—because so much shame and guilt are attached to it, because it has been suppressed and left unspoken for years.

The truth is a force of such magnitude that it demands to be known, one way or another. If buried, the truth will push its way to the surface. Denial or suppression of the truth will manifest as ill health, dysfunctional relationships, or financial problems. The truth does not remain silenced or suppressed comfortably. It may take a lifetime, but the truth *will* win out. As any good detective will tell you, even dead men tell tales.

I receive at least 15 frantic messages an hour from people desperately requesting help with their problems. By the time they contact me, they have sought out countless doctors, medical procedures, prescription drugs, you name it. They are often at a point of collapse—writhing in physical or emotional pain. The truth of their past is burning inside them like a house on fire. But they do not know that. They think they have "caught" some dreaded disease or virus; they think they are doomed to a life of misery and suffering.

We cannot live a lie and have peace. We cannot live a lie and have joy. True peace and joy are manifestations of living our personal truth.

As my story and the stories of thousands whom I have treated make clear, everything that happens to us is stored in our bodies and the energy fields surrounding them. Ultimately, health and healing happen only when a body/mind/soul wants, needs, and is ready to face the truth. Even after a lifetime of suppression, a body/mind/soul that is willing to release painful secrets can heal itself, a family, even a nation. What ultimately saves us is what we were certain would kill us—the truth.

I once heard a story about an aboriginal tribe that conducts a healing ceremony whenever anyone in the village is sick. The person with the high fever or the stomach ailment or the depression or the congested lungs sits in the center of a circle of all the villagers. The sick person is invited to speak the things *that have been left unsaid* by directly addressing those he felt harmed by or whom he had harmed with words or actions. What has been weighing on his heart that has never been shared? What dreams have been suppressed? The person speaks his truth. The villagers listen and acknowledge what has been said; they sit in the circle with the person who has been sick until that person is well.

The tribe knows what we as a culture have forgotten: *truth heals.*

MY LIFE OF LIES

I had no relationship with the truth as a child. I was raised— by both my parents—to lie and to live the lie. My father was warm, affectionate, and loving. Every night he would comfort me and talk to me and connect with me. I remember his smell: fresh shirts and whiskey and cigarettes. Daddy's hands loved me and coddled me and fondled me but not always in a healthy, nurturing way. Our relationship had a dark side—a side that fostered his constant admonition, "Don't tell! Don't tell! Don't tell!" I was taught to keep secrets, a terrible burden, especially for a child. Children know that secrets are dangerous. They know secrets can hurt them and the family they love.

There were times when Bad Daddy marched down the hall toward my room. This was our secret that would remain unspoken, suppressed, hidden. I was learning what I would later master—the art of bottling up and never expressing the truth. By the time I was three or four years old, the habit of lying was entrenched in the cells of my body, mind, and being.

My mother also taught me, by example, the skill of denial, further shaping me into an adept liar. She looked away, ignoring what was happening between my father and me. Because I was so terrified of her, I learned to lie in order not to displease her. I also learned to disappear into my lies.

As a teenager, I put out the message that I came from a loving family, that my mother loved and cared about me. The truth was that she hated me. She did not have the same disposition toward my brother; he wasn't female. Mother hated her own womanhood and projected that hatred onto me. Of course, I could not recognize that as a child. All I knew was that comfort, love, and understanding were not to be found in her arms. I do not remember a single instance when she held me, kissed me, or spoke loving words to me.

When we lie long enough, *the lie becomes who we are*. I became so practiced at lying that I was no longer aware I was doing it. I could not distinguish between the truth and a lie. I had learned that telling the truth was not safe; in fact, the truth was not to be seen or felt or heard.

By the time I was in my twenties, I wore the lie like a beautiful suit of clothes. I was an attorney like my father: married, accomplished, successful. I was picture-perfect or so I led everyone to believe. What I did not show others, and what

I barely admitted to myself, was that I was out of control—on a roller coaster of depression and manic acting out, drinking, and promiscuous affairs. My body became a minefield full of hidden problems I chose to ignore. Only when I was diagnosed with cancer did I decide to address the truth.

All my life I knew that I had been sexually abused—or I should say that "Cindy," my internal collector of these experiences, knew. Cindy was the part of my personality that housed all the memories of those events. I was not split off from Cindy as occurs in someone with multiple personalities; I had a strong mind, and Cindy and I stayed connected. She was a safe haven of sorts, a way I could disassociate a little from what was happening. Cindy will show up regularly on the pages of this book.

I "invented" Cindy when my father started abusing me. When I was very young, Cindy would tell me about the warm, fuzzy times with my father. As I grew older, the stories grew more frightening. I knew that certain stories, the very worst ones, she did not tell me at all. I did not want to recognize the truth of these memories, but eventually I didn't have a choice. My health depended on my knowing them.

My illnesses woke me up—as illnesses often do. All those battles and all that suppression of my feelings took their toll. As much as I was willing to lie, my body was not. You cannot argue with illness. You need your body to move about in the world, and, if it's not working, you are really stuck. I started off with throat ailments as a child and proceeded to develop sicknesses of all kinds: hypoglycemia, stomach problems, and allergies galore. Along the way, I added manic depression, promiscuity, and alcohol and Valium addictions to the mix—all before I finally woke up with a diagnosis of cancer at 25.

The truth took a long time to face. I had fabricated and invested myself in a life that was far removed from it. There were secrets I was never going to tell. I was absolutely certain those secrets would go with me to the grave, but I was wrong. My personal truth—my secret pain—finally manifested as cancer to grab my attention. Had it not been for cancer, the truth of my past might have remained buried and I along with it.

I wanted to live, and I was willing to do whatever it took to heal.

One day, at my wit's end, I stumbled into a massage therapist's office. As she began to work on me, she asked if I was open to "energy healing." I didn't know what that meant, but it sounded good, so I said yes. That began my awakening.

ENERGY

We live in a culture that is dying for the truth—literally. When we keep painful secrets or tell lies, we distort our energy fields, weaken our immune systems, pickle our organs, constrict our hearts, rattle our brains, and confuse our nervous systems. Lies turn the body into a toxic waste dump.

The principles of physics tell us that *energy* is the driving force of the universe and everything contained within it. In fact, our bodies and their surrounding systems are kaleidoscopes of energy.

From bottom to top—from the first energy center (root chakra) located at the base of the spine up through the seventh energy center (crown chakra) located at the top of the head—we consist of a complex system that receives energy from the world and sends out energy in what is intended to be a healthy in-and-out cycle. When balanced, the energy centers in the body are spinning vortices that keep us healthy.

We want our energy systems to function normally. We want them to be able to pull energy in to nourish and support us. We want free-flowing energy throughout every cell, tissue, and organ in our bodies.

Life experiences, emotional upsets, surgeries, accidents, and trauma of any kind can shock and impair our energy systems. If these experiences are not processed and released over time, a lack of energy flow in some area of the body may manifest as illness or other problems. Memories of painful events may be "forgotten"—denied or suppressed by the conscious mind as a means of coping with fear, sorrow, or rage. But the body never forgets because it stores those memories. The scream that wasn't screamed, the anger that was never expressed, the sadness that was stifled—all leave their mark.

Having experienced the painful episodes of my childhood and young adulthood, I am hyper-aware of the pain of others. For many who enter the field of healing, life credentials are as important, even more important, than theory or clinical training. Ironically, experiencing the problems of my early years gave me the perfect education in becoming a healer, though I did not know that at the time. If I had enjoyed a frolicking happy childhood without incident, I do not think I would have embarked upon this path.

HEALING THROUGH THE TRUTH

In my practice, people regularly come to me with a laundry list of health complaints. One man told me, "At 20 years of age, I started to have trouble with my cervical spine. I went to an orthopedic surgeon, then a chiropractor, then a dentist for jaw pain, and finally to a pain specialist." As I scanned his energy field, I found that the disturbances in his body, manifesting as chronic ailments, were *unexpressed screams*. He had stifled his feelings, which caused havoc in his body. His jaw was frozen in fear, just as mine had been for many years. Children need to scream when they are scared or hurt. But children who can't cry out or who are punished for expressing their pain must articulate it somehow, and their bodies bear the brunt of that pain until they do.

In my own quest for recovery, I spent years working with different sages, shamans, and healers. As my awakening began, the horrors that I experienced came to light. The unexpressed energy inside me screeched to get out. Over and over again, as various people worked on me, I heard these words inwardly shouting through my body, *Please don't hurt me, Daddy! Please don't hurt me!*

The truth could no longer stay down. It demanded a voice. The truth I had always known, but buried, burst out to the surface. The lie that almost killed me—the seemingly convenient and malleable lie—was no longer my salvation.

I wanted to live. The truth saved my life.

The lies we use to hide our truth sit inside us like time bombs; the sooner we are willing to dismantle the lies, the sooner we can heal. Telling the truth is an act of love—love for ourselves, for our lives, and for all those we love.

To heal, however, *it isn't necessary to remember all the horrific details that you may have suppressed.* When I urge people to get in touch with *their truth,* it might be, for example, just the fact that their childhood was pretty grim. A person doesn't need to remember that his father beat him black and blue and burned his hands with cigarettes. But if he wants to be healthy, he should stop kidding himself that he had the best dad ever. He must acknowledge the truth, at least to himself.

Knowing our own truth is crucial, but it may not be smart or even safe to confront others with it. Getting in touch with our memories is very freeing, but always use good judgment as to sharing the details of that truth with others. Laying it on others who "can't handle the truth" may only create more hurt and pain.

Forgiveness takes time—sometimes a lifetime. In many ways, I believe I have forgiven my parents for their failings. Still, as I worked on the early drafts of this book, I became aware that my mother was noticeably missing from the pages. My father was everywhere; my mother was a non-story, chillingly present by her absence. In the pages of my manuscript, I had recreated the same dynamic with my parents that had persisted throughout my childhood. I had to write about my mother as well as my father in order to heal. My hope is that telling the truth will help heal my lineage as well.

While the truth may mend our wounds, a disease process may have already started. The physical body may in fact need attention. I am a firm believer in integrated therapies and encourage those who have medical problems to seek immediate help for their physical condition from all sources.

Truth Heals reveals, explores, and illuminates how illness is a function of distortions in one's energy system caused by suppressed, denied, or forgotten truth; by emotional experiences that have never been addressed; and by painful traumas that have never been recognized or resolved.

Each chapter begins with a short excerpt (shown in italics) from a memoir I wrote many years ago while engaged in my own recovery. The book is set out in seven chapters, one for each of the seven major centers (*chakras*) in the human energy system. In each chapter, I discuss the specific emotional habits and resulting physical problems related to that area of the body, illuminating the characteristics of each center with stories drawn from my practice and examples from celebrities. Simple checklists are included to help you identify any problems in that area of your own life and body. These stories all illustrate, time and time again, how *truth heals*.

You will notice that I sometimes use the word *God* to reference my connection with the nonphysical world. I was raised as a Catholic, and so my childhood frame of reference was a Christian one. Today I don't identify with any particular faith but rather with elements of all of them. I frequently attend services at various churches and temples. I go wherever I feel a connection to Source, and I have found it in the most disparate settings: Evangelicals speaking in tongues, Benedictine monks chanting, Hindus meditating, Sufis dancing. I believe strongly that many paths lead to spirit and to wellness. I use the term *God* because it is the one I am most comfortable with, but for you it may be something different. Truth transcends belief systems; it is universal and accessible to everyone no matter what you call your Source.

It is my hope that you will meet and embrace your truth or the truth of someone you love in these pages and that you will be encouraged by what you read to do the work involved in healing.

May the truth set *you* free.

CHAPTER ONE

Is It Safe Here?

Mother glowers at me as she walks across the hardwood floor. What have I done to incur such wrath? I try to shrink, to minimize my existence. If I breathe only a tiny bit, maybe she won't notice me. I have learned to hold my breath for longer and longer periods. Can I make myself any smaller? Raggedy Ann looks at me and I look back. I mimic her wide-eyed stare.

Mother marches toward me. I panic, hold my breath, pretend I am as small and limp and lifeless as Raggedy Ann. I will not make even a peep. I hope this will save me. Mother's rage moves closer. Nothing can save me. I dissolve . . . disappear into nothingness. I look at my hands. They are gone. So are my feet. I float past the chandelier. I hover at the corner of the mantle and then come to rest on a beam. Everything looks different from up here. Nobody can hurt me. The woman marches back and forth below me. I fall asleep.

When I wake up, Raggedy Ann and I are back in the playpen. And the woman I call Mother is gone.

I was scared a lot around my mother. She was always angry, glaring with her infamous killer look or, in my case, "kill her" look that chilled me to the bone. When her eyes landed on me, they felt like cold swords piercing my heart. I coped by shutting down, disappearing into the air. My only defensive strategy as a small child was to leave, to float out of my body and around the room so I could hide from her cold glare. I didn't know what I had done to deserve her anger. Later I discovered my sin: being a girl who was loved by my father.

Mother. Half-Portuguese and half-Irish, Mother herself was the child of a very repressed and angry mother and an alcoholic father. Never was she "Mom" or "Mommy." The primal bond between mother and child had not formed between us. The picture-perfect Norman Rockwell image of a loving mother nursing her small child was never my reality. Mother despised my existence, and I lived in constant fear of her. As a child, Mother was mostly a woman to be feared. Today, as an adult, I see her in a different light—the product of her own painful childhood.

Mother was only 18 years old when she met my father, who had hired her to be his secretary. Handsome and sophisticated, he was 22 years her senior and a prominent lawyer and politician. Shortly after giving birth to my brother, their first child, Mother discovered that her new husband drank to excess, like her own father. She vowed not to have more children. But my father's insistence won out.

One summer night, having learned she was with child, Mother tried to end the pregnancy with a knitting needle—as her mother had done before her. Everything about sex and pregnancy disgusted her. It was distasteful, obscene, and stirred memories of illicit touching from her own childhood. She viewed pregnancy as even dirtier if the progeny turned out to be female. Girls were the source of all evil and seduced men into sin: this belief was central to my mother's view of reality. Unable to terminate her pregnancy, she carried me until the eighth month and then pleaded with the doctor to take me forcibly from her womb.

In my experience, her mothering was cruel, cold, frightening, and deeply unkind. She mothered how she had been taught. The idea that she had been anything but a good mother would have been inconceivable to her.

I am certain that my ability to leave my body began in the womb. A fetus is like a sponge, absorbing everything happening emotionally and physically with the mother. No doubt I knew in an unconscious, preverbal, but deeply sensory and excruciatingly painful way that my mother did not want me—a circumstance *anyone* would want to flee. But I was trapped in Mother's womb, unable to escape her hostility. The psychic pain of not being wanted laid the foundation for a distorted first energy center and my primal unconscious theme: *It's not safe. I don't want to be here.*

THE FIRST ENERGY CENTER:
ROOT CHAKRA

The first energy center, or root chakra, is the very foundation of physical existence. Located at the base of the spine, the root chakra's enormous influence carries our life force upward in our bodies and also downward through our legs, connecting us to the earth for grounding and support. Key root chakra issues are safety and trust, nourishment, health, home, and family. The areas at risk with an unbalanced first chakra are the adrenal glands, the base of the spine, coccyx, legs, feet, bones, rectum, immune system, and spinal column.

When the base energy center is distorted, a multitude of possible outcomes can happen. We may develop a feeling of being ungrounded, with the sensation of not really being here; poor focus and discipline; or fear, anxiety, and phobias. We may become restless or have an inability to settle down. Lack of organizational skills, feelings of abandonment, resistance to change, and low energy or lack of physical power are other indicators that the root chakra is not balanced.

When an energy center in the body shuts down, the effect is like sitting on one leg for a week: when we try to stand, that leg won't hold us up. The same scenario occurs with the body. We can't deprive it of fluidity and energy for long periods of time and not pay for it. When any area is compromised or blocked by painful memories or present circumstances, the body suffers.

A distorted first chakra can lead to the following physical problems:

- Eating disorders or malnourishment
- Adrenal insufficiency

- Problems with feet, legs, or coccyx
- Rectal or colon cancer
- Spinal problems
- Immune-related disorders
- Osteoporosis or other bone disorders

The root chakra gives us our sense of belonging. Any number of events at any point in our lives can cause imbalance or deficiency in this chakra. Loss of a job or relationship, a car accident, moving house and home, threat of or actual violence, or a natural disaster—all these can shock us into pulling up roots and throw us out of balance.

In the case of a major tragedy like the World Trade Center attack in 2001, the trauma can last long after the event. Many survivors described an extended period of intense emotional suffering and felt incapable of returning to normal life and the job they held before. Many also described being gripped with terror, jumping at the slightest noise, and not being able to settle down, sleep, or focus. These are all indications of a distorted first chakra.

Such survivors commonly have their first chakras "blown out" by fear and terror. They often say they feel like they are "not here." And, in fact, at the level of the root chakra, they are not. The shock has displaced their attention and awareness; they are "out of their bodies." As one female survivor described it, "I don't know who I am anymore. I don't enjoy the things I used to. I can't even go into Manhattan."

BE HERE NOW

Presence is a chief characteristic of an integrated first chakra. By "presence" I mean that all of me is really here, in my body, at this very moment. Those with root chakra problems are often not present in their lives. It is fairly common in our culture to be absent or semi-absent much of the time. "Beam me up, Scotty," the humorous phrase from the hit TV series *Star Trek,* found its way into common vernacular because it expresses the age-old desire to vanish into thin air when the going gets really tough.

Many of us leave our bodies without realizing it. Think of all the times we drive on the freeway and arrive at our destinations unaware of the trip. We function on autopilot—so absorbed in thought that the car seems to have driven itself. How often do we wash the dishes, go to the gym, or shop for groceries when we are really somewhere else in our minds? Our culture's reliance on technology has likewise disassociated us from the present—and from nature and each other as well. When we replace human interaction with technology, we feel even further disconnected. Think how often we sit in front of our computers and only realize how sore we are at the end of the day after not having moved for hours at a time.

Many of us "split" from our bodies when we were very young. Like a reflex, we protected ourselves by pulling out when danger approached. This splitting, or disassociation, made sense when we were children, when the only way we could survive the shocks that assailed our immature nervous systems was to "check out" of our bodies. As adults, we want to break this pattern of disassociating from our bodies when we are frightened or distracted because, in reality, we can only protect ourselves if we stay. When we are not present, we are literally unable to take care of ourselves because no one is home.

A textbook case of the results of root chakra discord is Patty Duke, before she received appropriate treatment. A hard-working and talented actress who was not yet 13 years old when she became a star playing Helen Keller in *The Miracle Worker*, she was born to an alcoholic father and a mother who was an undiagnosed manic depressive. Her first six years of life were filled with her parents' fighting. After her

Don't Check Out . . . Stay Here

It may well have been our strategy to exit energetically
when things got overwhelming for us as children.
But learning to stay present and deal with what
is in front of us is the task of a healthy adult.
If you notice yourself wanting to "check out,"
take a deep breath, plant your feet on the ground,
and tell yourself, "It's safe to be here in my body right now."

father left, her mother's violent rages meant her home was still an unsafe place. When she was eight years old, her life was taken over by her managers, John and Ethel Ross, who took her from the proverbial frying pan right into the fire. John Ross sexually abused her, provided free access to prescription drugs and alcohol, and had her do their housework and cooking.

Patty escaped from the Rosses by marrying at age 18, but then plunged into severe depression, bouts of mania, suicide attempts, anorexia, drug abuse, and alcoholism, all symptoms of first chakra imbalance. Her second marriage lasted all of two weeks before being annulled. In her third marriage, she suddenly found herself the mother of five boys. After the break-up of that marriage, at the age of 35, she was finally diagnosed with bipolar disorder; it was a huge relief for her to know she had a treatable condition. She went back to her real name of Anna Marie and wrote her autobiography, *A Brilliant Madness;* giving expression to her feelings likely helped her reestablish connection with her roots that had been disconnected when she was a child. Today, she is able to maintain a stable life as a spokesperson and activist for mental health awareness.

Another example of first chakra "not wanting to be here" was Ashton Kutcher's experience as a young child and teen. Ashton came to fame as the not-too-bright character Michael Kelso on Fox's *That '70s Show.* His parents, both struggling factory workers, divorced when he was 13. Not wanting to take sides with one or the other parent or hear bad news about his twin brother, Michael, who was born with mild cerebral palsy, Kutcher kept himself disconnected by staying too busy to feel—a classic way to "get out of Dodge" when it's not safe to be here. When he was 13, his twin developed heart disease. Told by the doctors that Michael had only hours to live, Ashton went out on the hospital balcony, ready to jump so his brother could have his heart—a state of mind evidencing loss of connection to his own physical safety. Just in time, the doctors announced that a woman had died in a car accident and a heart was on the way. Was Ashton so "not here" that he would have jumped? Thankfully, the trauma passed, and today he is regrounded and present, maintains a career in movies and as a television producer, and is a supportive stepdad to his wife Demi Moore's daughters.

EATING DISORDERS

I could have been a poster child for first chakra distortion. I had every sign of a poorly functioning base chakra by the time I was 18. Always battling anxiety, I increased my Valium intake every year. I jumped at the slightest noise and had trouble sleeping. After barely recovering from a cold, I would immediately catch the flu. Although I wore a size four, I was sure I was overweight and lived on Diet Coke, eggs, and grapes—a classic unconscious attempt to "get out of here" by not eating.

Most eating disorders are primarily a first chakra issue having to do with the basic need to be here and attend to the body's need for nourishment. Individuals whose sense of safety is compromised or who frequently have their boundaries crossed by a powerful "other" may begin to feel they have no control over their destiny. They zero in on eating as the one aspect of life they can control.

Jennifer was 21 years old when her father brought her into my office. She had been struggling with anorexia/bulimia for nearly a decade and was running out of options. Jennifer's basic sense of home, family, and safety had been deeply injured by her parents' divorce when she was only three years old. While both parents loved her very much, the constant bouncing back and forth between two homes and the hostility between her mother and father made Jennifer feel like a pawn in their game of war. From the time Jennifer was three until age eight, her mother moved into a new house nearly every year. Adjusting to new homes, new friends, new neighbors, and new schools time after time left Jennifer feeling rootless and unstable. When she sought comfort from her mother, she was told, "You are so lucky. You have two parents who love you and two great houses to live in. You have more than I ever had as a child."

Jennifer's mother was model-thin and proud of it. Her father, on the other hand, constantly battled with his weight. At mom's house, where Jennifer was admonished to eat sparingly, the cupboards were always nearly empty. Set mealtimes did not exist, and they certainly never cooked together as mother and daughter. At her father's house, food was in great supply. Her father loved to eat big meals and often snacked well into the evening.

Jennifer's eating disorder began at 11 years of age when her mother married a man who didn't want to be burdened with a stepchild. Jennifer began to flip-flop between starving herself and overeating. She became more and more self-conscious and confused about eating, especially when her stepfather took to calling her "fat ass" whenever she ate anything rich or sweet. By the time she was 13, Jennifer had begun to purge after eating. Even after she moved in with her father full-time at age 14, she continued to eat sparingly and often faked eating for her dad's sake—all the while getting thinner and thinner. The Jennifer in my office still looked like that 14-year-old; she was so frail and wan, I had to keep reminding myself she was actually 21.

As I began to work with Jennifer, I noticed that she had a distorted first chakra. She had little conscious connection with her body. Like many of us who have suffered from eating disorders, Jennifer felt her world was out of control so she exerted control over the one thing she could: what she put in her mouth. This was Jennifer's unconscious reaction to the trauma. Starving herself also gave Jennifer the illusion that she could disappear from her situation. Not eating was a way of not feeling present, a physical expression of "I don't want to be here."

When her parents became aware of her condition, they each blamed the other, adding ammunition to their constant warring. Each accused the other of not being a good parent. Jennifer barricaded herself in her bedroom, put her headphones on, and escaped into music. Her parents sought help for Jennifer from medical doctors, psychotherapists, and treatment programs. Nothing worked and her condition continued to worsen. The final straw for Jennifer came when her father kicked her out of the house for dropping out of college. No longer welcome in her father's home, she turned to her mother. But her mother did not want her either; she had recently had a baby and was simply too preoccupied with her second husband and new family. Without a home to call her own, Jennifer shut down completely and embarked on a chilling eating strike.

As we worked together, I began to see that Jennifer was a deeply sensitive and artistic girl who had no sense of where she belonged in the world. She got attention from her parents when, as she said, she "screwed up," which she did with regularity. In my earliest sessions with Jennifer, I could extract nothing more than "I don't know" in answer to my questions. I also noticed she could not recognize a single good quality in herself. She could not remember the last time anyone talked to her about anything other than her eating disorder.

I often see this narrow viewpoint in clients and a number of techniques that I have studied involve broadening their perspective. I look beyond the disease process to a fuller picture of the individual and, using focused intent, bring into view their innate perfection. While Jennifer may have lost sight of her perfection in the throes of her illness, it was my function to keep it firmly in mind. I concentrated on her higher qualities and emphasized her strengths—her resilient attitude, her courage to face her truth, her honesty about her feelings. Beneath her "I don't know" was a cascade of tears that poured out with confessions she had bottled up for years. She admitted that her eating disorder was the one thing that was hers and hers alone. When her father—whom she considered the more loving of her parents—asked her to leave his house, she felt as if the ground beneath her feet opened up to swallow her.

As she began to realize that she could be safe by "being here," present and grounded inside her body, she realized she could rely on herself rather than others. The work we did together transformed her belief that "the world is unsafe" into its opposite: "the world is safe when I am present." With the help of an eating disorder specialist, she started eating as a way to acknowledge her increased sense of self. She realized that eating kept her *here* and that *here* was a place she wanted to be.

Jennifer is not alone. Eating disorders are pervasive among girls and women. Paula Abdul, Victoria Beckham, and Mary-Kate Olsen are just three of many celebrities who have publicly admitted to struggling with eating issues. For these women, having their pictures splashed across magazines and TV screens increases the pressure to be perfect. Even Princess Diana, the most photographed woman of the late twentieth century, struggled with an eating disorder. Singer/songwriter Fiona Apple became anorexic after being raped outside her home when she was only twelve years old. She has said she wasn't anorexic out of a desire to be thin, but as a reaction to being raped. When it's not safe to be here, an eating disorder seems to provide a way out. As Paula Abdul, who is a spokesperson for the National Eating Disorders Association, has said, "Eating disorders really have nothing to do with food, it's about feelings."

HOLDING ON TO ILLNESS

Acknowledging our own truth frees up our energy systems, thus enhancing the way they function. We need well-functioning energy systems in order to have strong bodies— healthy blood running through our veins and arteries; properly functioning organs; and vigorous lymphatic, nervous, and immune systems. Yet many people wait until death is at their doorsteps before they admit the truth; others would rather take it to their graves.

Audrey had been confined to bed with chronic fatigue syndrome for more than 11 years. Before she became ill, Audrey maintained an active dermatology practice in Los Angeles. Driving two hours every day between her private practice and several clinics, she felt like she "lived on L.A. freeways." When the cell phone became central to her life, she found that her driving time on the freeways became her window for returning client calls, talking to her stockbroker, and counseling her bereaved mother, who had recently been widowed for a second time.

"I call those my grueling days," she told me. "I spent half

the time daydreaming about moving away to a small town so I could slow down. But at that point, I couldn't imagine how I would live on a smaller income. My husband and I were already living beyond our means. We even put our wedding on a credit card."

Three years into the marriage, upon returning from a Caribbean vacation, Audrey came down with a bad case of the flu. After two weeks, she got worse instead of better. When her condition failed to improve over the next two months, her doctor began an extensive series of tests. Ruling out an infectious disease first, her growing medical team looked for indications of an autoimmune disorder but found nothing diagnostically significant. After six months in bed, Audrey was given the catch-all diagnosis when nothing else fits—chronic fatigue syndrome. A year later, her husband filed for divorce and moved out of state. Audrey began getting disability benefits and gave up all hope of returning to work. She sold her car in a telling move that ensured she would not get into the "fast lane" again any time soon.

When I examined Audrey, I found her first chakra circling counterclockwise (a healthy one moves clockwise). Moving in the wrong direction, it was sending out energy rather than taking it in. Her energy field also held a great deal of fear.

Audrey had been born with a birth defect in her hip that required two surgeries when she was only two years old. Surgery is a traumatic event for anyone, especially for someone so young. Surgery shocked her fragile young body and created a lot of fear about her safety. Audrey often felt that nobody was there for her and that she had to act like a "big girl" long before she was ready. Her parents were not very supportive during her early years, and only when she was sick did Audrey feel her parents' love and attention.

As I continued to scan her delicate body, I saw another scene: Audrey surrounded by a group of menacing men in some foreign location. "When was the last time you traveled overseas?" I asked.

"Oh, god. Years ago. Just before I fell ill, before the divorce. We went to Jamaica."

"Did something happen there?"

Audrey then described an incident that had occurred the night before she and her husband returned to Los Angeles. While walking back to the hotel after a last-minute shopping flurry that found her out after sunset alone, she'd been cornered by a gang of locals. Afraid they would pull her into a nearby alley and rob or rape her, she screamed until several passersby came to her aid. She recalled that critical moment as one in which she'd felt frozen and completely unable to act on her impulse to run. With no ability to leave the situation physically, her energy system had reacted by going into a "fight or flight" pattern and her energy system "fled," setting up the dynamic of an immune system moving into retreat.

Audrey volunteered that her life wasn't as bad as one might think, despite the fact that she spent 75 percent of her time in bed and left the house only once every two weeks when a friend took her grocery shopping. When I expressed shock that she had endured this condition for 11 years, she told me she had adjusted her definition of happiness to fit her circumstances, and insisted that she was content. She felt blessed by the care and attention her mother now lavished on her.

I explained to Audrey that she no longer needed to be confined to a bed to feel safe and loved. When we examined her current belief system, she realized that her old fears and reservations no longer fit. The fear of being accosted in a dark alley was a dim memory. She also didn't need to fear becoming trapped by a stressful job or an expensive lifestyle any longer, as she had long ago abandoned both. In short, after 11 years, she no longer needed to fear getting well.

For Audrey, however, a clear payoff or "secondary gain" came with remaining sick: it fulfilled her heart's desire to be taken care of. Although recognized as a talented and capable businesswoman, she really hungered for the loving care she had missed as a small child. When I gently suggested to Audrey that she might want to be taken care of, she was horrified. She told me it was preposterous to believe that she would "want" a disease. But from everything that I could see, she wanted her disease more than she wanted her health. Being ill meant she would receive the attention she so desperately craved. Admitting the truth—that at a deep unconscious level she didn't want to heal—might well have restored her health.

The last time I saw Audrey, a friend brought her to one of

my workshops. Her illness was so far advanced that she couldn't even sit up in her wheelchair for more than a few minutes at a time. She looked ravaged, gray, and ashen—a 45-year-old woman in the body of an 85-year-old—a tragic commitment to illness in an unconscious quest for parental love.

HEALING CANCER

Hans first came into my office after undergoing surgery for colon cancer; he had already begun the initial phase of chemotherapy. A hard-driving man, Hans was a senior vice president in sales who enjoyed all the trappings of success. As

Pay Attention . . . Accidents Are No Accident

*Accidents are the body's mechanism
for getting our attention.
Whether it is a car accident, sports injury,
or we trip headlong into a wall,
it is an indication that we are not really in our bodies,
that something has taken our focus away.
Accidents slam us back into reality, sometimes literally.
It's the way our bodies and the universe say,
"Hey, pay attention! You're important!"*

I scanned his energy field, I saw a scared little boy behind his competent facade. He had worked hard all his life to prove himself and was an accomplished overachiever. Like many overachievers, however, he was underloved.

Hans explained in that first session that he had a history of serious accidents. I was not surprised to hear this, as his first energy center was not fully functional. Like so many clients I see with distorted root chakras, the lights were on, but no one was home. Accidents are frequently a hallmark of someone who is not fully present in his body. The number of accidents Hans had experienced as a child, and the number of car, skiing, and bike accidents he'd had in his teens, twenties, and thirties, made it clear that Hans was not a man who wanted to be here. He confessed that his wife was very worried that he was headed for the "big" accident that would kill him. He was also restless and could not sit still—two other characteristics that may indicate someone is out of his body more than he is in it. Hans was very concerned about the fact that he had not yet responded to his chemotherapy. He was worried about dying. I began by working to reduce Hans's fear level so that he could sleep at night.

After a number of sessions, I gently asked Hans about his childhood. In a flat, unemotional voice, he recited his history. He had grown up in Sweden, his parents were professional people, and he was the third of six siblings. Although his parents had been quite well off, they had not wanted so many children. Because Hans was bigger than the rest of the children, he had been the target of abuse. Starting at age two, his father beat him with a belt and punished him on a regular basis by locking him in cupboards for hours at a time. His mother had not breastfed him, and he received no nurturing, affection, or care. Hans's primary memory of childhood was, "I was always hungry."

His father further crushed Hans's big spirit by repeatedly calling him "the slow one." When he was shipped off to live with his aunt and uncle at the age of six, he still couldn't read. The uncle, his father's brother, continued the beatings. At the age of nine, the source of his reading problem was discovered: Hans needed glasses. By that time, however, the damage had been done. Getting sent off to boarding school at age 11 only solidified his feelings of abandonment. His self-assessment was by then firmly set: *I am really not okay.*

Anxious to get away from his family, Hans moved to the United States when he was 18 and shortly thereafter married an American. When his wife left him a few years later, he was shattered. This abandonment duplicated his early painful experience of rejection by his parents.

Abuse of any kind is damaging, but even more so if inflicted by one's own family or tribe because it shatters our basic sense of place and safety in the world. Planet Earth, Hans had learned, was a very unsafe place to be, and he was still living that energetic imprint. Scenes of his childhood unconsciously played inside him like a movie, sending the message over and over again: *You're not wanted! Leave!*

Abuse and trauma distort our energy fields and show up

in our bodies as illness and in our lives as all manner of emotional, financial, and interpersonal dysfunction. In this case, Hans's base chakra bore the brunt of the pain he had suffered as a child. That dysfunction impacted the adjacent area where the colon is located, and his colon housed all the painful, unpleasant energies of his childhood.

By guiding Hans's attention to his base center, we were able to release much of the old negative energy. All the beatings, disdain, and name-calling he had suffered at the hands of his father had remained in his body as "terror energy."

How did the truth heal Hans's colon cancer? After 40 years of suppression that developed into illness, he admitted in the privacy of my office those experiences from childhood that he had never told another soul. This truth freed him to be opened energetically. Speaking the words out loud—his truth about his fear, anger, shame, and sadness—allowed him to purge the energy and the illness from his body. The suppression of the truth had nearly killed him. As he began to understand the relationship between what he suffered as a child and the illnesses, accidents, and pain he had created, we were able to remove the blockages that had prevented his healing.

As we cleared the residue of unexpressed screams and tears, the possibility opened for his chemotherapy treatment to work more effectively. As is common in my experience, once an energy system is freed of the negative energy that has shut it down, medical interventions that previously failed begin to work. In Hans's case, his colon cancer ultimately healed. He stopped having accidents. To this day he remains healthy.

Often more than one area in the body tries to compensate for shocks to the system. Hans's solar plexus, the seat of self-esteem in the body (see page 63), was also distorted. While the truth helped heal his colon cancer, further healing was needed to overcome the shame and sorrow of feeling unworthy and unwanted.

Healing is always a process. To balance the body/mind, we must pay attention to our body's messages and assess our beliefs, letting go of those things that no longer serve us. Hard work on Hans's part was required to make healing changes in his life. First, he had to see the connection between the pain of his past and his current health. I recommended meditation to help him develop clarity and anchor himself in the present moment. I also suggested he resume his former hobby of gardening, as it would help him gather more energy and form a better connection to the earth.

A BALANCED FIRST CHAKRA

A fully integrated and healthy first chakra is associated with trust and safety, security and survival, and connection to family and community. An individual with a strong base feels at home in his or her body, is well grounded in physical reality, and makes the statement, "It is safe, and I want to be here now." He likely has a strong will to live and emanates vitality and life force.

A great example of someone with a functioning, fully

integrated first chakra Is publicly admired talk show host and philanthropist Oprah Winfrey. She exudes vitality, is connected to her family (which is the world), and is fully present and grounded. She has done much to heal from the abuse she suffered in her early years. As she has said, "We are not what happens to us; we get to choose *what to do* with what happens to us." Her safety comes from within, and she embodies abundance and trust in the world.

CHECKLIST

To determine the state of your first energy center, honestly answer the following questions:

1. Have I experienced traumas like major illnesses, accidents, surgeries, abuse, or shocking events?
2. Do I often "absent" myself from routine tasks? Am I in another world when I am showering, cleaning, driving, exercising?
3. Do I have any of the conditions listed on pages 16–17?
4. Is my immune system healthy, or do I get one "bug" after another?
5. Is it easy for me to retain my focus, or am I anxious or restless?
6. Do I have low energy?
7. Am I disorganized in my personal space or neglectful of my body?
8. Do I seem to have excessive fears or phobias?
9. Am I unreasonably resistant to change?

After considering these questions, if you suspect that your root energy center is not working optimally, spend time reflecting on which of your past or present experiences made you feel unsafe, out of control, or powerless. Don't discount the effects of prenatal difficulties or surgeries. Also, bear in mind that you may very well have had traumatic experiences as a child that you have repressed and don't recall—a normal response to abnormal situations. Although we often need to repress events as children, as adults we can seek support to deal with the traumatic fallout.

Let me be clear: *it is not necessary to vividly recall or relive an event to heal from it.* We repress certain experiences because they are too painful or too dangerous. All that is really required for healing is an awareness of how we feel now. If we suspect that our emotions today come from unresolved past experiences, we need to bring the idea of those events into our consciousness without worrying about the details.

Being grounded in our bodies gives us the experience of "I am here, and I am safe." Presence is essential for health because it is so easy to become ungrounded. Just watching the news can throw us into a state of panic. A wonderful way of literally reconnecting our bodies to the earth is to spend time walking barefoot on grass or on a sandy beach. Alternately, take a walk through a park, go hiking in the wilderness, or sit with your back against a tree. Yes, you can *be here now.*

CHAPTER TWO

Shame, Shame, Go Away

In kindergarten, I showed my little friends all the secret things I had learned at Daddy's knee. Well, not his knee, exactly. These secrets were special, too delicate for classroom show and tell. My friends were fascinated all the same. The nuns at school never spoke of such things. Neither did my mother.

The first chance I had to practice what I had learned from Daddy was on my 30-year-old judo instructor the year I was 15. Afterward, he said to me, "Where did you learn to give head like that?"

Blowjobs were more than a specialty; they were my raison d'être. A good blowjob could secure a coveted part-time college job, help score an A from a law school professor, and land that corner office at the law firm. Ah, yes, the law firm. I climbed the ladder on my knees. From associate to junior partner to senior partner in a record two years, I was never more than a blowjob away from the next rung.

I expanded my specialty practice. Opposing counsel and even judges were not immune to my charms. But it was my clients, those men of means and influence who came to me for legal help, who were my personal favorites. Never could I resist a man in need, and many a client who walked through my office door reeked of need. Every one of them reminded me of Daddy. They came for advice, but I gave them much, much more.

In an ideal world, childhood is a time of love, nurture, play, comfort, and safety. Our parents are guardians, charged with the responsibility of caring for and protecting us. As children, we are curious about everything, including our bodies. It is natural and innocent to explore our physical selves through all of our senses. Children who are touched, caressed, and embraced in appropriate ways and tended to with loving care develop a clear sense of self because the attention they receive is characterized by both clarity and safety. Children raised by parents with clear boundaries naturally develop appropriate boundaries of their own. They know how to say "no" if something doesn't feel right. They learn the natural flow of appropriately giving and receiving pleasure.

My father awakened me to the pleasure principle when I was very young. I loved him; he was my whole world, but I did not understand the confusion I felt when hands that had touched me in loving, nurturing ways suddenly felt invasive. I didn't understand the urgent, frenzied gestures or why his voice and his face changed into something frightening. The look on my father's face after one of those "episodes" was one of deep regret, remorse, and uncomprehending horror. He knew he had done something very wrong but did not understand why this terrible urge had seized him.

I do not know how far back in my father's family the incest secret extends. Such secrets are explosive, destined to erupt sooner or later. Shame—old, ancestral shame—has tremendous power. If not dealt with and healed, the pattern tends to repeat. As a child, my father had been the target of a sexual predator in his own family. The sexual abuse completely disempowered him, as it does all children. Sexual abuse is not as much about sex as it is about power. My father had no say in what happened to him and years later perpetuated the trance of shame and powerlessness with me.

That the "sins of the fathers" manifest in the lives of their progeny is evidenced across varying cultural and economic lines. The behaviors we think of as "sinful" often stem from the lies we tell ourselves or from the half-truths and outright distortions we have been spoon-fed by our families. More often than not, the process by which these lies persist is quite unconscious. Nonetheless, the process is hardly innocuous because it is the lie that makes us sick. Such distortions have an energy all their own and can profoundly influence the way our lives unfold.

Look at talented actress and pop singer Lindsay Lohan, who has been working since she was a Ford model at the age of three, and her dad Michael, a onetime actor, businessman, and investment banker. Michael has a history of addictive behavior. Sentenced for securities fraud, he spent three of his daughter's preteen years in prison. In 2005, he was sent back to prison for two more years for "aggravated unlicensed driving" and attempted assault. Lindsay, carrying on the family tradition, has been arrested twice for DUIs and both times was found to be carrying cocaine. Her father had passed on his behavior pattern to his oldest daughter, who has since done the requisite stint in rehab for drug and alcohol addiction. Estranged from her father since her parents' divorce, Lindsay has reestablished contact with her dad, who cleaned up his act some years ago and now works to help others who are still in the throes of addiction. Lindsay has admitted that she has her work cut out for her when it comes to beating her own addictions.

We know, of course, that heredity plays a role in addiction and that a cross-generational pattern of denial does as well. Once an addict stops denying and pretending that his use and abuse patterns are "normal" (i.e., not a problem), his awareness can expand to see what was previously hidden from view—his role in bringing on the unfortunate circumstance. Only then can he be honest with himself and speak the truth. These steps are crucial if he is going to experience growth and actually change the behavior. Michael Lohan, by being authentic and transparent, turned his "embarrassment" into a fierce commitment to telling the truth, unraveling the family lie and reversing an energetic pattern that has become so entrenched over time that it masqueraded as a family "curse."

Every single one of us has a dark side—those parts of ourselves we deem unlovable or that society condemns. As children we get messages that some of our impulses are not okay: "Don't do that or mommy won't love you." Love is withdrawn when we misbehave, are too exuberant or noisy, or cry too much, too long, or at the "wrong" time. Experiences that are scary or painful but remain unresolved add more dense energy to the mix. All these little moments in time instill repression and self-rejection that bloom into the dark side of our personalities. For most of us, the dark side is an inconvenient but not debilitating phenomenon. But human nature has quite a range of expression and the dark side can grow into psychopathic proportions, like that of O. J. Simpson or even Charles Manson.

The more we try to deny or avoid these undesirable aspects, the more likely they are to erupt in unexpected and embarrassing ways. When Mel Gibson was pulled over for drunk driving in Malibu, the press had a field day. Not only had his dark side surfaced as drunkenness (as we will see, substance abuse is almost always a second chakra issue), but the alcohol had also loosened his tongue. The anti-Semitic comments he made to the arresting officer generated quite a scandal, especially in light of criticism from the Jewish community that his film *The Passion of the Christ* was anti-Semitic propaganda, and was further fueled by his father's inflammatory views on an "exaggerated" Holocaust.

Substance abuse and addiction relate to the emotional reality of the lost child and connect to the second chakra. The addiction—whether to drugs, alcohol, food, sex, or other substances or behaviors—serves as a bridge between the conscious, competent self (Mel Gibson, world-renowned actor and producer) and the part of us that did not get our needs met in childhood (Mel Gibson, the sixth of eleven children whose fundamentalist Catholic father ran his household on "severely moral grounds") and has no choice but to expose repressed discontent (Mel Gibson, inebriated and uninhibited). In this way the addiction itself is a powerful pointer that can lead us to see, feel, and speak the underlying painful truth that allows the healing to begin. But until we take up the task of unearthing our own truth, we are vulnerable to periodic acting out when our dark side surfaces.

Prejudice stems from attitudes and beliefs we learn when we are too young to examine them critically and make up our own minds. Until such beliefs become problems with clear costs, we are unlikely to become motivated to examine and change them. Becoming aware is almost always the crucial first step to knowing the truth, and this often involves a startling or unexpected event that jolts us out of our denial. We come closer to the truth when we look at racism, for example, as an expression of our collective dark side—the unexamined, unhealed, repressed side of all of us who live in a society that condoned oppression of one race by another not so long ago and still harbors us/them, superior/inferior attitudes toward members of our own species.

When one person tells the truth, it has a healing effect on all of us. No act is beyond the reach of forgiveness and healing. We are all part of the unified field of energy; we are all connected. We know the truth when it is spoken. We feel the ripples of truth go out into the world and touch people's lives. We could even say that the entire universe breathes a little easier when one person speaks or acknowledges the truth and thus dismantles old lies.

THE SECOND ENERGY CENTER: THE SEXUAL CHAKRA

When our understanding of sexuality and personal relationships gets distorted at an early age, that damage registers in the body. The sexual abuse I endured created disturbances in my second chakra—the energy center in the body that is located several inches below the navel. This center, which is the seat of sensuality, sexuality, emotion, and our inner child, governs the way we relate in groups, how we establish boundaries with others and within ourselves, and how we find pleasure. The very essence of human interaction—learning to give and receive—comes from this center.

If the second chakra is distorted, we may develop poor boundaries and wind up attracting people who invade them or whose boundaries we invade. Or we may fall into victimizing others or feeling victimized ourselves. We may become overly seductive, manipulative, ambitious, dependent, martyr-like in behavior, or a sex, drug, or alcohol addict. We may compromise our ethics for sex or money or power; become greedy and hoard money, or the complete opposite—manifest financial problems, even poverty.

People with distorted second energy centers may experience a variety of physical problems, including:

- Sexual dysfunction, impotence, frigidity, or promiscuity
- In women: fibroids, endometriosis, pelvic inflammatory disease, menstrual dysfunction, ovarian cysts or cancer
- In men: prostate problems or prostate cancer
- Inflammatory bowel disease, ulcerative colitis, Crohn's disease, diverticulitis
- Appendicitis
- Chronic low back pain or sciatica

- Bladder problems
- Urinary problems

Victims of sexual abuse frequently suffer from distorted second energy centers and the associated conditions and illnesses. Although rarely acknowledged, children are actually very sexual/sensual beings. When the pleasure principle is prematurely activated in a child, pleasure becomes linked with shame. The cocktail of emotions that is stirred inside the child—a sickening mixture of fear, confusion, excitement, terror, and sometimes pleasure—is potent and damaging. When the child is told *not to tell*, an unholy alliance between pleasure and shame is created.

Initially, what the child feels is the perpetrator's shame. The perpetrator leaves his shame in the child's energy field and the child takes it on and later adds more of his own.

Shame is a dense energy. Children wear shame as if it belongs to them, as if it is them. The longer they don't tell and continue to wear the coat of shame, the more likely they are to carry that shame into adulthood and unconsciously find ways of shaming themselves and others, over and over again. Adults like my father, trapped in the trance of shame, may be unconsciously drawn to a child's innocence and pure spirit. They may not remember their own abuse because they have repressed it. However, the twisted, shaming energy is alive in them, spinning like a vortex through their energy fields and the cells of their bodies. A literal force field in the body and subconscious mind, this shame then provokes them into acting out the abuse and repeating what was done to them.

My father abused me until I was 12, when he then stopped completely. The part of me I called "Cindy" bore the brunt of the abuse and kept the more perverse acts from my conscious awareness, but I could do nothing to stop the truth's inevitable expression. With no other outlet for my repressed rage and shame, I began to act out sexually at 15, becoming a wild adolescent and later an even wilder adult. I ricocheted between manic and depressive episodes, drank heavily, acted promiscuously, and developed illnesses.

Acting out was my soul's loud and desperate cry for help. My mother was embarrassed by my outrageous behavior, which was not in keeping with her proper Catholic upbringing. She took me to a psychiatrist and said, "Fix her." The psychiatrist, more voyeur than therapist, seemed to take pleasure in the stories of my sexual escapades. He never made the connection between my behavior and the possibility of sexual abuse, and I never confided in him.

THE POWER OF SHAME

For many of us, it takes years to gain the courage to speak or acknowledge the truth. Some of us who have come out of silence are able to act as guides for others. We lead others across the chasm of fear, self-judgment, and shame so they may express their truth that has been aching to be recognized for years.

Shame wants out, but it doesn't know how to get out. The child wants to tell, but can't. The child wants to scream, but dares not. So this urge to express is suppressed. If we don't heal the shame, we are doomed to repeat and perhaps even perpetuate its effects. To distort an old children's rhyme: *Shame, shame, go away.* But it won't, unless the truth of the original shame is safely expressed and thereby transformed. Otherwise, shame will indeed *come again another day,* in different, more inventive forms.

The eccentric entrepreneur, aviator, and filmmaker Howard Hughes is a dramatic example of someone who paid a deadly toll for shame. The son of wealthy parents who both died when he was a teenager, Hughes inherited a sizable portion of his father's multimillion-dollar fortune. He became one of the wealthiest men in the world, with a voracious appetite for sex, money, and success. He was a notorious womanizer and targeted the silver screen goddesses of his day, among them Katharine Hepburn and Ava Gardner. Early in life, Hughes decided he wanted to be the best—the best pilot, the best movie producer, the best golfer. As head of his own company, Hughes Aircraft, he designed and built innovative aircraft and set world records for speed. In Hollywood, Hughes became a force to be reckoned with. But by his 50s, Howard Hughes had begun a descent into obsessive-compulsive behavior.

In *The Aviator,* a biopic about Hughes, we are given a window into the possible genesis of his eccentricities when we see his mother sponging him down in a tub of water. This scene is quite disturbing, with possible sexual overtones as Howard is clearly too old to be bathed by his mother. Her actions suggest a woman who was also unbalanced and compulsive about cleanliness. If Howard was unable to express his discomfort when she did this and instead pushed his feelings out of awareness (as most of us do), those intense feelings were bound to erupt in bizarre ways. The scene sets the stage for his obsession with cleanliness and order and his later rebellion against it. His compulsions, obsessions, addictions, and sordid death gave tragic testimony to the power of shame to wreak havoc in terrifying ways—the central theme of a distorted second chakra.

David is another example of someone whose shame manifested as illness. He arrived in my office concerned about a prostate antigen test that indicated the potential for prostate cancer. As we began working together, I discerned that David lived with a great deal of shame. After I prodded him gently, he confided a history of chronic promiscuity. Although he loved his wife, he had engaged in an affair when she was pregnant with their first child. Initially, his wife was unaware of this first "fling," but she later discovered his infidelity. The hurt this caused both of them overshadowed the delight David felt about becoming a father. Yet, try as he might, he could not stop his philandering behavior.

I saw that David had an unbalanced and excessive second energy center. A good deal of pain was energetically trapped in his body from the hurt he had caused his wife. He was anxious to bring an end to his behavior, as the most recent incident had become quite a scandal. While his wife was pregnant with their fourth child, a child he avidly wished for, David had an affair with a woman who lived in their small town. When the trouble came to roost in his hometown, David knew he was out of control. To make matters worse, the "other woman" was notorious for sexual escapades and their little town buzzed with the gossip. David was horribly ashamed and deeply upset by this, and his wife was so furious and hurt she began to talk about divorce.

When I asked David if he had a sense of why he behaved in a way that was so upsetting to both himself and his wife, he didn't have an answer. He clearly didn't know what motivated his behavior. He just felt ashamed of his actions. Shame begets shame, so the more shame he felt, the more he took actions that shamed him even further.

David simply shrugged when I first asked him about his childhood. Later he shared that the sudden death of his mother when he was six years old propelled him into a place of deep sorrow, where he felt an unquenchable need for comfort. He attached himself to any warm female who came near—teachers, aunts, his father's numerous girlfriends—but never found the lasting comfort he needed. A simple yet powerful thought had taken over his mind, *if I had loved my mother more, she would not have died.* He somehow felt he was responsible for his mother's death, which caused him a great deal of shame and contributed to the sense that no matter how much he loved a woman, he would always lose her.

As we worked to release the sorrow and shame stored in his energy field, David began to make the connection between his promiscuity and the loss of his mother. As an adult, he saw how his actions were an attempt to fill the need of a child for a warm maternal presence. David's almost rabid desire for the "warm body" of a woman—any woman or lots of women—diminished as he began to connect the dots. He realized that he could take care of himself and that he did not need women to survive. The pain and sorrow he felt at the loss of his mother had never been expressed or released, only suppressed. In a child-like way, David had managed to stave off the feelings of loss and grief by clouding his life with a succession of affairs.

The realization was profound for David, and he was able to break his sexual addiction. As we cleared his field and his

Water Heals

Water can be healing. Pour a bath, add one pound each
of sea salt and baking soda, and soak for 20 minutes or more.
Allow all your old feelings and thoughts about your past
to be drawn out by the salt water.
Imagine all of that guilt or shame dissolving into the bath
and being washed away as you say the words,
"I speak the truth and reclaim my true nature.
I am pure. I am clean."

body of the negative energy over the next few months, David's prostate got better. He reported that subsequent antigen tests showed continued improvement.

Although his prostate concerns had diminished, David came back to see me when he started to realize he might have a problem with alcohol. I gave him a questionnaire from Alcoholics Anonymous (AA) and his answers were telling. He fit the profile of an alcoholic, but at first did not want to admit to the serious nature of his drinking. Alcohol was deeply woven into the fabric of David's life: his friends, family, and business buddies all drank. Sobriety would be a radical break from a habit he had come to call a "friend." But David knew he was in trouble and he made the decision to stop drinking and to start attending AA.

As a former addict myself, I know that abusing a substance of any kind is an action taken to mask uncomfortable feelings. At first, our addictions make us feel good. The negative feelings go away and we feel on top of the world, capable of dealing with anything. Eventually, the addiction begins to affect our lives in negative ways and, over time, exacts a heavy toll.

QUEENS OF SEDUCTION

As an adult, I confronted my mother about my father's abuse. At first, she admitted it might have occurred. Later, she denied knowing about it, but as a child I remember seeing her more than once watching us through a crack in my bedroom door. She despised us both; she assumed I, a little girl of six, had seduced her husband—the proverbial Eve tempting

Adam and bringing about the fall from Paradise. Daddy always said, "Don't worry about your mother, she doesn't love us and she doesn't understand." But we were both afraid of her and her wrath.

Women who rely on seduction usually have an excessive and distorted second energy center. Marilyn Monroe was every man's dream woman—someone who epitomized seduction. However, she had a history of failed marriages, including those to playwright Arthur Miller and baseball great Joe DiMaggio. She also attached herself to unavailable men through a series of unfulfilling affairs and was reputed to be President John F. Kennedy's mistress. Marilyn was emotionally dependent on men, and her boundaries collapsed around them. She suffered from depression, fear of abandonment, and the tandem fears of losing control and being controlled.

What Marilyn Monroe had, and what our mothers and many women still have encoded in their cellular memory, is the entrenched belief that a woman is nothing without a man. This belief holds that no matter how hard a woman tries or how much she achieves, she will never be equal in value to a man. This belief system does a great disservice to both men and women by denying the feminine principle in men and the masculine principle in women, rather than recognizing the need to balance these principles in both genders.

Although Marilyn displayed all the classic symptoms of a dysfunctional and unhealthy second chakra, she epitomized beauty and sexuality for many. The focus of the world's media attention was on the way she looked. If Marilyn's only currency was her image, she could not feel loved for herself but only as the world saw her: a sexual fantasy rather than a real person. Marilyn was reputed to be a bright and talented actress, yet her natural gifts were rarely the focus of media attention. When a person's value is so strenuously attached to her appearance, she dies inside.

A more current version of Marilyn can be seen in the life and death of Anna Nicole Smith, the Playboy playmate who married oil tycoon J. Howard Marshall, a father figure many decades older than her. Abandoned by her father as an infant, Anna Nicole's early years were spent in trailer parks fighting with her mother, failed relationships, and strip bars. Possibly abused, her distorted second chakra led her to use sex and seduction to attract attention. The older she got, the more insecure she became about her beauty, just like her idol Marilyn Monroe. Like Marilyn, Anna Nicole had a string of men; like Marilyn, she alternated between pure seduction and helplessness. Also like Marilyn, her relationships suffered from her need for companionship competing with her resentment about being overly controlled.

By identifying herself so strongly with Marilyn Monroe, Anna Nicole actually connected energetically to Monroe's patterns of periodic self-starvation, drinking, and drug use, which also connected her to Monroe's tragic early death from an accidental drug overdose. After her son's accidental death from a lethal combination of methadone and antidepressants, Anna

Nicole was undoubtedly self-medicating for depression. Anna Nicole wanted to be like Marilyn Monroe her whole life and sadly died in a similar manner.

THE QUEST FOR HEALING

By the time I was 25, a young attorney making my way up the ladder, I began to suffer all manner of gynecological and blood-sugar disorders. Then, a life-threatening diagnosis of cancer threw me into a tailspin.

Looking for answers, I found what later became my life's path when I received my introduction to alternative medicine in the office of a massage therapist. For the first time, I began to reflect on my difficult childhood. How could I reconcile the two sides of my father? How could I come to some kind of understanding of my mother's refusal to love me? It seemed impossible, but I knew it was necessary in order for me to get well. I was guided to one complementary medical practitioner after another as I put together the pieces of an excruciating puzzle, bit by bit.

Our wounds always lead us on quests—consciously or unconsciously—toward healing. In my life and in my practice, I have seen this again and again. Clients come in with an illness or combination of conditions that are often terrible. They are as desperate for help as I was. If I can help them to recognize their disease as the way their body is trying to draw their attention to a deeper truth, their healing can begin.

Alicia, a 34-year-old insurance executive with a fast-paced and demanding life, came into my office after being diagnosed with ovarian cancer; she was looking for alternatives to heal her cancer. My first observation from scanning Alicia's energy field was that she had many symptoms that indicated post-traumatic stress syndrome predating the cancer. She had poor boundaries, insomnia, and recurring nightmares.

Most of Alicia's attention was focused on her appearance—an exhausting and never-ending pursuit for perfection. Alicia was accustomed to filling all her free time with a rigid exercise routine so she could stay as thin as possible. Excessive exercise and dieting had divorced her from her own natural rhythms and bodily processes. At the same time, she was intent on becoming a fabulous gourmet cook to impress her husband and friends.

Alicia's relationship with her husband of seven years was troubled; arguments were the norm. After her husband had been drinking one night, he demanded sex. She said no, but he violently forced himself on her. Ashamed, she told no one about the rape and explained her injuries by saying she had fallen down a flight of stairs. She wanted to leave her marriage but was afraid of bringing on more psychological or physical abuse. She had been raised to believe that men came first and that she had to do everything to "catch, please, and keep a man." During our first session, she blurted out that her older brother had sexually abused her when she was eight years old. When she told her mother, her mother had replied with that old nugget of wisdom, "Boys will be boys." She went on birth control pills at 13, diet pills at 15, and antidepressants at 17.

Our work together addressed Alicia's dilemma on several levels. First, I assisted her in opening her pelvis energetically, where the first and second energy centers are located. This entire area of her body was shut down. Layer after layer of negative energy—in response to the abuse she had experienced as a child—remained in her field, blocking a positive flow. I worked to repair the subtle layers that made up the energy field surrounding her body and to lift out, sift through, and release the heavy burden of fear, guilt, shame, and self-blame stored there. At the same time, I helped Alicia to raise her awareness about the core beliefs that had trapped the unresolved trauma in her body. The family in which she was born and raised had anchored a belief in her body and mind that abuse was somehow normal, that it was natural for a female to be dominated and subjugated. Unconscious thought patterns like these are etched in the deepest and oldest regions of our brains.

Alicia's second chakra was not bringing in energy in a healthy clockwise way, but was moving in the opposite direction. Her energy center was sending out a beacon signal: "Because I am female, I am prey, worthy of assault." In this respect, Alicia fashioned her own reality, literally projecting her childhood expectation of danger onto the adult world. Alicia had re-created a male aggressor—her husband—to duplicate her experience of being abused by her brother. In the same way as solving a puzzle, I follow the energetic lead of my clients, piecing my way through the maze of their beliefs until I arrive at a deep inner place where they are stuck. I carefully help them over that point to the other side, where a sense of freedom and expansion can occur. In this way, I worked on Alicia's patterns, using a delicate technique I learned from a powerful shaman.

During her early sessions with me, Alicia could not answer my simple query, "What does Alicia want?" The first time I asked that question, she responded with, "I don't know. I've never thought about it." This was the truthful answer of a woman who had always thought that the entire focus of her life should be on what her man wants. As her healing progressed, some of her old beliefs changed, and she began to focus on making herself a priority. Slowly but surely, her cancer markers declined. She eventually left her husband and returned to school to pursue a degree in theater arts. Five years later, follow-up scans continue to show the cancer in remission. Alicia began dating and healing the way she related to men.

Practice Saying No

If you have said yes *when you meant* no,
the simple act of saying no *is empowering.*
You honor yourself, and you honor others
when you tell the truth about what's right for you.

A BALANCED SECOND CHAKRA

People with integrated sacral centers enjoy touching and being touched. They are comfortable giving and receiving enjoyment, love, money, and material goods. They know how and when to say no and have a sense of internal balance between their masculine and feminine qualities.

A healthy second chakra is a fertile place—an engine of creative possibility that allows inspiration to flow through the body. As the seat of the inner child and emotions, this center also hosts our creative and generative impulse. I am speaking of creativity in the widest sense of the word here. Creativity is not limited to the arts. Men and women express creative inspiration through their entire energy field and body/mind in a host of different ways every day.

An example of someone who has taken tremendous strides toward integration in this area is Sir Elton John. A piano prodigy at the age of three and a musical force since the 1960s, he is one of the most successful artists of all time. He is not only a singer/songwriter of ballads but also a flamboyant arena rocker who wields a piano instead of a guitar. The special Grammy award-winning version of "Candle in the Wind" that John performed at the funeral of his good friend Princess Diana became the biggest-selling single of all time, with the proceeds going to The Diana, Princess of Wales Memorial Fund. That year he also lost another close friend when Italian designer Gianni Versace was murdered.

Elton John battled alcohol and cocaine addiction for years, as well as struggling with bulimia and with overspending that created financial difficulties. When his young friend, Ryan White—the hemophiliac who was expelled from school after being diagnosed with AIDS from an infected blood transfusion—died, John said, "Sitting with Ryan's mother Jeanne at his bedside as he lay dying in April of 1990 was one of the most gut-wrenching experiences of my life. I knew I had to do more." As the first step in that direction, John finally admitted to himself he was powerless over his addictions and took a year off from his career to clean up his act. After getting out of rehab, he founded the Elton John AIDS Foundation, one of the world's leading nonprofits for supporting HIV/AIDS prevention education programs and direct care services to people living with HIV/AIDS. As he says in a letter on the Foundation's website: ". . . the most meaningful part of my public life is my work as a humanitarian in the global effort to end the AIDS epidemic." He had learned to channel his own problems into positive giving.

CHECKLIST

To determine if your sacral center is in balance, ask yourself the following questions:

1. Have I had any of the illnesses listed on pages 44–45?
2. Have I used sex to get what I want in abusive or seductive ways? Do I routinely fake orgasms?
3. Do I have any addictions: food, drugs, alcohol, sex, or behaviors that injure me or others?

4. Do I have money problems?

5. Do I feel that I give and give and give and get nothing back?

6. Do my friends complain that "everything is always about me" or that I am too needy?

7. Do I feel chronically alone, lonely, or abandoned by people?

8. Am I self-defeating and feel as if I can't accomplish anything?

9. Am I uncomfortable saying "no" and establishing good boundaries for myself?

10. Do I act out irresponsibly or try to blame others?

If you answer *yes* to any of these questions, you may want to seek help finding better balance. One way of cultivating a habit of self-nurture and self-care is to immerse yourself in water on a regular basis.

Another way to nurture yourself is to play music that duplicates the sound of the ocean—a good way to calm your body and environment. You can also clear and charge this chakra by walking in the moonlight.

Bringing awareness to tendencies that have become second nature is very powerful. Simply become aware of your patterns, without guilt or shame. Once you have awareness, the best ways to accelerate your healing can be sought out. In some cases the right path to take will simply appear. Remember, the first step to healing is always awareness.

CHAPTER THREE

Is Winning Everything?

Our family camping trip had barely begun when Daddy decided that he and I ought to go off and do a little fishing. I feared what "fishing" might involve but swallowed my fear and did as I was told.

That afternoon, Daddy's familiar stroking became strange and urgent. I knew the signal. By then, I also knew just how to relieve his growing anxiety, to meet his ever-increasing needs. I dropped to my knees as he held my head tight by my braids. But this time I couldn't seem to get it right. He became frantic, pulling me closer and closer. I started to panic. Suddenly, he pushed me to the ground and climbed on top of me. I couldn't breathe. When I cried out, he put his hand over my mouth. I shrank beneath his heaving body and felt nothing but the flies on my arms as I watched the treetops sway in the breeze above me. The smell of sweat and blood mingled with the smell of grass and Daddy's clean khaki shirt.

Afterward, he wept.

I was nine years old.

The day after the rape, I fell out of a tree and was rushed to the hospital. I spent the next three weeks in a hospital bed. The nurses called it *recuperating*. Daddy kept a safe and reserved distance between us for the rest of the summer. He had taken what he needed, just as it had been taken from him when he was a child.

How does it feel to be overpowered? Like you've just been steamrolled. Like you don't exist. Nobody sees you; all that exists is that person's *need*. You are in the way or you are the way. Just like that, what you thought was yours is gone.

I was disempowered by a man who attempted to take solace in his daughter for the misery he felt from his own childhood and his marriage. My mother stood by and let the abuse happen because she had been taught by her mother to pretend that "her man could do no wrong." "We are all victims of victims," a wise person once said. We are wounded by the wounded.

Being raped by my father at the age of nine devoured my emerging identity. The "I" of my fledgling, fragile sense of I-*dentity* was subsumed. Identity is our stamp on the world that says, *This is me, I am this. That is you, you are that.* When our identities emerge, we begin to gain clarity and strength about who we are, what we like, and how to take a stand.

Before the rape, the boundary of where my father ended and I began was already blurred. I'd always known how to breathe in his sadness, to comfort him when he seemed frustrated, to soothe him when I sensed something was wrong between him and my mother. I cared about my father and understood him in a way that Mother never did. We were bonded—an unhealthy bonding, but it was all I had. The fear and rage I felt from the abuse and my mother's refusal to deal with it were kept underground. There was no speaking it, no feeling it, no acknowledging it in any way, at least not consciously. After the rape, the little part of me that I had left vanished. It was stamped out, swallowed up by the vortex of Daddy's pain and shame and weakness. There was no "I." There was only Daddy.

THE THIRD ENERGY CENTER: THE POWER CHAKRA

The devastation that occurs as a result of a trauma such as rape often shatters the fragile third energy center. This is the body's primary power center, the source of will, purpose, and action. The third chakra is the seat of self-worth; our self-esteem and personal power emanate from this vital center. Located at the solar plexus midway between the navel and the sternum, the third chakra corresponds with the center of our metabolic fire—that which fuels us and gives us vitality. From this center we harness our energy and convert it into action. The seat of our will is also in the third chakra. Strength of will and personal power are developed when the solar plexus functions according to its design.

When the third energy center is excessive or deficient, some of the resulting medical issues may include:

- Problems with the pancreas, including diabetes and hypoglycemia
- Digestive difficulties, such as gastric or duodenal ulcers
- Liver problems, including cirrhosis, hepatitis, and liver cancer
- Hiatal hernia
- Gallstones
- Hemorrhoids
- Varicose veins
- Problems with the spleen

The pancreas, located in the area of the third chakra, processes and assimilates emotions and regulates blood sugar. An unbalanced third energy center can cause hypoglycemia (low blood sugar), a condition that is the opposite of diabetes. Often, those with hypoglycemia can't express their emotions clearly for fear that safety or love will be lost if they say what they think. They may worry a lot, and many are perfectionists. Their interior statement is: "There is not enough love or safety or approval." They are always waiting for the enemy that they fear is everywhere.

Truman Capote, one of the 20th century's famed writers, is a good example of someone who seemed to have no trouble saying what he thought, but whose unbalanced third chakra and misuse of personal power cost him dearly. Capote demonstrated this imbalance early on in his turbulent career when he lost his copyboy job at the *New Yorker* for insulting a famous author at a public reading. He was known not only for his outrageous behavior, but for a tendency to backstab even his closest friends. In his famous nonfiction work, *In Cold Blood,* Capote tells the story of how two drifters massacred a wealthy Kansas wheat farmer and his family in 1959. Capote gained access to the killers while they were imprisoned on death row. He developed a close friendship with one of the men, even going so far as to promise he would do everything in his power to seek a stay of execution. But when the killer's fate remained unresolved and Capote's book project was left hanging, Capote withdrew his support on the killer's behalf. Much ethical hue and cry was made over Capote's actions at the time, which led to the execution of his supposed "friend," but criticism did not sway him nor did it diminish the success of his book.

Butterflies in Your Stomach

Butterflies or the fluttery feeling of energy in the stomach that we normally "read" as anxiety, excitement, or fear is actually a sign that the third energy center is preparing itself for an approaching challenge. The best remedy is to ask yourself,
What am I afraid of? And what can I do to protect myself?
Bringing feelings to conscious awareness is the best way to change them.

If we wonder what effect misuse of personal power can have, we can learn a great deal from Capote. On the one hand, he represented himself as a friend and competent writer; on the other, he was motivated by self-interest and failed to deliver on important promises and projects. He never wrote anything of real merit after *In Cold Blood,* and his descent into miserable alcoholism played out publicly on the talk show circuit. He died in 1984 of a diseased liver. I would suggest that putting ambition ahead of what he knew to be honorable caused his downfall. When we act in ways that betray our integrity, we poison our bodies, minds, and spirits.

INWARD COLLAPSE

An unbalanced third energy center may be expressed in either *outward push* mode (the aggressor) or *inward collapse* mode (the victim). Co-dependent relationships are fertile breeding grounds for this push/collapse dynamic. One person plays the role of "can-do" while the other acts out the "can't-do"; both are disempowered. Each person has a stake in his distinct role and works to maintain it—consciously or subconsciously—by reinforcing the sense of identity derived from his role. Both can have serious health consequences.

Those with collapsed third energy centers often feel doubtful, indecisive, and lacking in self-confidence. They may complain of low energy and of an inability to follow through. They may feel like victims of circumstance or pushovers, unable to interact positively and powerfully in the world, or even to "just show up." As acclaimed filmmaker Woody Allen is often quoted as saying, "Ninety percent of success is just showing up."

Maureen came into my office suffering with diabetes, but her real ailment was a collapsed third energy center, the result of giving her power away. *Di-a-be-tes*—die a bit at a time—was the way I would describe what had been happening to Maureen. Thirty-five years old when we met, she had developed Type 1 diabetes after her father's death 17 years earlier.

She saw her father as the one parent who really loved her. After he died she was saddled with her mother, with whom she had an ongoing power struggle. The notion of sweetness died with her father and, slowly but surely, Maureen had been dying a bit at a time ever since.

Within the family, Maureen's mother was considered a powerhouse. She was an accomplished woman who never rested between achievements. Maureen was her cheerleader, the one who sat on the sidelines and offered applause. Her mother rarely acknowledged or encouraged Maureen. She made sure Maureen would fail by saying things like, "That's a great idea, but how are you ever going to do that?" Maureen felt lost before she began and often thought, *why even try?*

Maureen's mother came from a long line of domineering women who dictated rules and choices for their children. She commanded Maureen to attend family functions, and Maureen felt she had no choice but to obey. She never expressed her true feelings around her mother, but simply went along with whatever her mother wanted. She was unaware of how deeply she had swallowed the rage she felt at being controlled.

Although genetic predisposition is a factor in diabetes, from the perspective of energy medicine the roots of the disease can be traced to control issues. Common issues include bottling up unpalatable emotions and overbearing control by a parent. Among Maureen's earliest memories were scenes in which her mother ordered her to sweep the porch and then ripped the broom out of her hands for not completing the job fast enough. As much as Maureen tried to please her mother throughout her life, she could not. Her mother was never satisfied, grinding into Maureen the belief that she could never do anything right. Maureen became disempowered, unable to love herself or to attract someone into her life who could care for her. She consistently battled internal forces that duplicated the external battle she had with her mother—trapped between accepting and rejecting herself, between feeling in control and out of control, between wanting to assert her will and feeling like giving up.

When I examined Maureen, I saw a shield of energy that appeared as a significant constriction over her pancreas. The message I received from her pancreas was, "I control my diabetes, but I am getting tired." The war with her mother had been projected onto the disease.

Maureen's energy field held a vector of force just off her left shoulder, indicating that an opposing psychic energy was coming in from someone—in this case, from her mother. A vector of force is a conscious or unconscious negative intent that is sent our way. Her mother's message to Maureen was: "You will do as I say." This vector of energy was literally creating a physical imbalance inside Maureen; she seemed to be holding onto herself for dear life with a quiet, unrelenting tension. She used tremendous internal energy to hold in her emotions—strangling them until she no longer felt them.

The physical constriction that is caused in a diabetic pattern extends not only to the pancreas but also to the circulatory system. Not surprisingly, high blood pressure leading to a heart attack is the major cause of death in those who suffer with diabetes.

Western medicine regards diabetes as controllable but not curable. Like many diabetics, Maureen was on a schedule of insulin shots. In my experience, both Type 1 and Type 2 diabetes can be dramatically improved through a change in core beliefs, the release of stored emotions, and changes in diet and exercise.

Maureen began to turn around her health when she confronted her true feelings about her mother. I assisted her in modifying some of her core beliefs, particularly the idea that she had to say *yes* to her mother regardless of her own needs or wishes. I supported her decision to forego family functions that she did not want to attend. Although her mother disapproved, Maureen needed to have a life of her own. As our work together continued, she began to see that she had been abdicating her power to her mother her whole life. She had allowed her mother to hijack her personal will. Gradually, her blood sugar levels began to improve.

Initially, Maureen found it difficult to relinquish her disease because she had become attached to it, as if it were an old friend. The same was true for her reluctance to move away from her mother. As much as she hated how her mother treated her, at least it was familiar. Finally, after one particularly obnoxious family day, she'd had enough. She applied for a company transfer and moved to another state.

Shocked and angry, her mother shared her bitter disapproval with everyone she could, but Maureen adjusted quickly to her new job and home. The move marked her first act of *individuation*—of separating out who she really was from what her mother needed her to be—and it did her a world of good. At my suggestion, Maureen sought out a support group to help heal her core beliefs as well as to integrate a more holistic approach to life. She also took up Pilates exercises, which puts a great deal of emphasis on healthy breathing techniques. Learning to breathe more fully allowed Maureen to relax her body and let go of some of the constriction that had become second nature.

Over the course of several years, Maureen's insulin dosages were reduced under the direction of her physician. The last time I spoke to Maureen, she had graduated from insulin shots to oral medication. She felt free from both the shot regime and her mother. I told her to continue to visualize herself as entirely free of diabetes, knowing that the template of perfection lies just beyond our view.

A famous example of someone who may have a third energy center distortion with an inward collapse is James Frey, author of the bestselling memoir *A Million Little Pieces.* The first book of its kind ever recommended by Oprah's Book Club, Frey's memoir instantly climbed to the top of the *New York Times* best-seller list. Frey was on top of the world until the authenticity of his "memoir" was questioned. When the Smoking Gun website brought public attention to substantial fabrications in Frey's life story, the facade began to crack. Initially held up as something of a maverick and a shining example of one addict's recovery, Frey was defamed just a few months later. Live on the *Oprah* show, Frey was publicly reprimanded for lying in print and deceiving both Oprah and his million-plus readers.

By his own admission, Frey is a compulsive overachiever. Compulsive overachievers are almost never balanced people. Winning at all costs while sacrificing integrity is a common trait in those with unintegrated third chakras. In the case of James Frey, his unquenchable appetite for approval and success over-rode his commitment to the truth.

LIVER TOXICITY

The largest organ in the area of the third chakra is the liver. The United States Center for Disease Control does not mention liver toxicity in its list of the ten leading causes of death. I believe it should. Oriental medicine considers a toxic liver the main cause of all disease.

In our society, a *stagnant liver* is alarmingly common, and liver function can be impaired long before any sign of trouble. Our livers process and filter everything we put into our bodies;

proper functioning of the liver is crucial, especially given the growing toxic burden of the modern world. As stagnation in the liver increases, toxicity builds and can show up anywhere in the body, manifesting in myriad disease or pre-disease conditions. Signs of a stressed liver include hemorrhoids, varicose veins, jaundice, skin eruptions, and abdominal swelling, to name just a few.

The energy dynamic we often see affecting the liver is persistent, repressed anger. When I scan someone's field, a stressed liver looks like a hot boiling cauldron—fiery red with blobs of yellow. Frequently, anger turns inward and eats its subject alive. Those with toxic livers may have disconnected from their heart's desires and are not being true to themselves. They often feel victimized and repeat stories from the past about their victimizer while refusing to alter their behaviors or beliefs. They are stubbornly committed to staying angry, and therefore unconsciously sabotage themselves. Rarely are they aware of the need to take responsibility for their own actions.

Roger had been a successful trial attorney for many years when he arrived at my office with a diagnosis of cirrhosis of the liver. On the liver transplant list, he came to see me hoping that I could help buy him some time. Roger was a small man but gave the illusion of being bigger. He was very talkative and wanted to tell me all about himself. He said proudly that if he had a personal motto it would be: "Don't get mad, get even." He had long eyelashes and fine features and mentioned that he had been taunted and abused as a child for being "too pretty."

His father was a hard-driving, hard-drinking man who built dams and bridges around the world and was frequently away from home. His mother resented her husband's absences and took out her frustrations on Roger.

At the age of seven, Roger's mother sent him to boarding school. While away, Roger was sexually abused by an older student. Unable to defend himself and terrorized by the thought of someone finding out, he had simply swallowed his rage. He was always trying to prove that he was *more man* than the next and as capable in business as his father. Everything he did in life was an attempt to gain his father's approval, but he never succeeded.

Roger felt rejected by both of his parents and repeated that dynamic by rejecting women who cared about him. He confessed that he had never remained in a successful long-term relationship. He was consistently unkind to his girlfriends as a way of testing their love for him. He masked his anger with drinking, harbored old resentments, and had no forgiveness for himself or others. He was overly hard on himself if he made a mistake. He lacked self-confidence even though he could move around the courtroom in complete control during a trial.

Roger was resistant to my suggestions for anger release work. He would say, "By God, I'm not going to let *them* do this to me anymore." The irony was that *he* was the cause of the destruction he feared. Displacing blame onto others and "the world" is a common characteristic of those with poorly functioning third chakras. Roger was the kind of guy who would get mad at the cop who gave him a speeding ticket.

When cancerous cells were found in his liver, Roger was denied a transplant. He saw this as confirmation for his belief that the world would always reject him, and, sadly, he died a few months later.

Roger is an example of someone with outward push or an excessive third energy center. He tried to make himself bigger to compensate for unconscious insecurity. He refused to consider changing his belief system and was unable to see the relationship between his stored anger and his illness. Although he seemed tenacious, his aggression was mostly taken out on himself, and his liver paid the price.

We can improve the state of our liver with simple lifestyle changes: reducing fatty foods, limiting our intake of drugs, alcohol, and over-the-counter medications, eating pesticide-free organic food (pesticides are a major cause of liver disease), avoiding exposure to chemicals, and not blaming or attacking others.

OUTWARD PUSH

In North America, we live in an outward push culture characterized by an intense desire to succeed. We are bombarded with technology that helps us do more, faster, better. Cell phones, computers, fax machines, PDAs, "on-demand" TV, and "instant messages" have taken over our lives. We are pushed beyond our limits on a daily basis.

At the cultural level, outward push manifests in all kinds of distortions. We say we demand truth and justice, but we accept exaggeration, rumor, innuendo, and flat-out lies fed to us by the media in the name of "entertainment." The line between truth and fiction has always been somewhat subjective, but cultural trends such as reality TV make it more difficult than ever to trust our eyes and ears to relay what is true.

Donald Trump epitomizes someone on outward push. Even his signature "You're fired!" hand gesture on the reality TV show *The Apprentice* demonstrated the aggressive stance of a person whose *modus operandi* is "push it to the max." Not unlike Midas, whose touch turned things to gold, everything Trump touches turns into the biggest and the best. Whether the project is a large-scale real estate development or designing his personal living space, the Trump Touch means *over-the-top*. He would be the first to agree that his taste is opulent and his personal style dominating, even overbearing. He is famously outspoken and sees himself as the ultimate successful businessman, putting his name on everything from watches to hotels, from casinos to golf courses.

People with distorted third energy centers in outward push mode will overtake and overwhelm others to gain power. The excessive solar plexus can be seen in type A personalities—people who are aggressive, pushy, or impatient. In the extreme, these people are perpetrators of abuse who prey on others. Frequently, they even try to "push" time itself.

Like many who are disempowered as children, I learned as a young adult that I felt safest when I was in control of others. I used seduction and manipulation to accomplish that goal. Although I was very much the aggressor as a young adult, putting my own agenda first, I never confronted issues or people directly.

I was a control freak and on *push* at all times. At a conference I attended, a woman's climbing team on its way to the Himalayas sold T-shirts with the slogan: A WOMAN'S PLACE IS ON TOP. I bought several of those T-shirts and wore them until they were in tatters, never conscious of my need to make that slogan come true. I was a *sidewinder*, using my power in covert ways. As a lawyer, I was a power and adrenaline junkie, and took great pleasure in slaying my opponents, who never knew what hit them. The energy from my solar plexus fanned out from behind, wrapped around them and, before they knew it, I had won.

Far from being healthy and balanced, I did not have the ability to seek cooperation. I can truthfully say I stole power.

Pushing Time

Do you push to accomplish the impossible
in a short amount of time?
Of course, we can't literally expand the minutes in a day,
but we sure do try.
If you always feel there's not enough time,
relax . . . take a breath . . .
love yourself for what you've already accomplished.

Working in a man's world, I rarely made friends with women. I was afraid of them; they all reminded me of Mother. Men were my game, and I always won. Being the best at everything was my reaction to my parents taking my power away from me. I was never going to let that happen again. But I was completely unaware of the deep rage I harbored at myself, at my parents, and at the world.

Anger in someone on outward push can be a deadly and corrosive force. Jane came to my office complaining of ulcers. She was a very angry woman, yet she was just as disconnected from her rage as I had been from mine. She had developed hemorrhoids in her 20s and painful varicose veins in her 30s. By the time she arrived in my office, the pain had progressed to her stomach.

She was also in a lot of emotional pain because her husband had left their marriage and was living with his new girlfriend. During the course of their 15-year marriage, she was a career sales associate and he was a bank manager. She had been the superior breadwinner and rubbed her husband's face in that fact regularly. He had brought two young children to the marriage, but she never embraced the children and had always treated them as an inconvenient nuisance. She wanted her husband all to herself. While he loved her a great deal, Jane's husband found her more and more difficult to live with and was deeply affected by her cold and uncaring manner with his children. He had hoped that she would love him and his children, but the children had no safe harbor with her and, in fact, felt more and more rejected by her over time.

One night her husband turned her down when she wanted sex. She was furious. "How dare you reject me!" she said and threatened to kick him out of the house. Much to her surprise, he actually moved out of their home and into a trailer. Jane was devastated. She felt certain he would come back with his tail between his legs. However, her husband had no desire to return to her critical, cold ways and found a new girlfriend within a month. Two years later, Jane was still bitterly angry, filled with rage and jealousy, and desperate to get her ex-husband back.

It took Jane a long time to make the connection between her rage and her ulcers, varicose veins, and hemorrhoids. Through our work, she connected with the depth of her anger, the roots of which predated her anger at her ex-husband. When Jane was a little girl, her father repeatedly rejected her for not being a boy. Regardless of what she did or how hard she tried, she was never good enough in her father's eyes. Deeply hurt and wounded by his rejection, she repeated her father's pattern with her husband and stepchildren. She became the rejecting parent and rebuffed her husband's children to such a degree that he felt rejected too. Her behavior eroded any feelings of connection he had to her.

I suggested to Jane that it was not too late to love her stepchildren. After some resistance, she sought out her stepson and spent several weekends with him and her new grandbaby. She began to realize that she must first learn to give love in order to receive the love she so desperately craves.

A BALANCED THIRD CHAKRA

When our third energy centers are fit and healthy, we feel able to take action. Our intentions are clearly focused. Those with vibrant third energy centers claim their power and stand in it. They have no need to demand or ruthlessly take power from someone else. Power flows to them because they know who they are and who they are not. These people can accomplish a great deal in the world.

An inspiring example of someone with an integrated third energy center is Halle Berry, the first African-American woman to win the Academy Award for Best Actress for her role in the movie *Monster's Ball*. Berry, the child of a white mother and African-American father, was a shy young girl whose father drank and abused her mother before he left when she was four years old. Kids teased her about her mixed color at school, yet she chose to become a beauty queen, fashion model, and then an actress. While filming a television show, she fainted on the set from undiagnosed diabetes and wound up in a coma for a week. When she woke up, she embarked on a healthy diet and exercise lifestyle. Now she says that diabetes turned out to be a gift. She said, "It gave me strength and toughness because I had to face reality, no matter how uncomfortable or painful it was."

That pain included her attempted suicide after her first marriage failed. It was a vision of her mother finding her that stopped Berry. In *Parade* magazine, she said, "My sense of worth was so low. I had to reprogram myself to see the good in me. Because someone didn't love me didn't mean I was unlovable. I promised myself I would never be a coward again." Halle Berry may have come from a place of desperate inadequacy, but her will and resilience have overcome the distortion in her third chakra. She now lives her truth without bending to what others think and has learned how to manifest her desires, overcoming her diabetic condition to have the baby she so wanted in her life, even after 35 negative pregnancy tests. In an interview in *Hello* magazine she said, "I have never been in better physical and emotional shape, and I'm happy in my personal life—what a novel idea!"

A few considerations for obtaining a balanced third chakra are:

- Live your truth without regard for what others think.
- Take responsibility for your words and actions.
- Acknowledge that you have a choice and the ability to manifest your desires.

CHECKLIST

If you have concerns about whether you have imbalance in this area, answer the following questions:

1. Am I prone to a condition listed on page 64?
2. Am I able to acknowledge and move through my feelings of anger and resentment without blaming or verbally attacking others?
3. Is jealously eating me up?

4. Do I feel I can cooperate with others as a team player, or do I invariably need to hog the limelight?
5. Do I chronically push myself and others to get things done? Do I try to "push" time itself?
6. Do I try to control others or events?
7. Do I have a habit of standing with my arms folded in front of me, above my waist, in an effort to protect my solar plexus?
8. Do I frequently feel overpowered by people I am with?
9. Is winning everything?
10. Do I require outside approval to feel okay about myself?

To support an increase in energy, vitality, and connection to self, I often recommend that people spend a portion of their day in the sun, preferably in the early morning or just before sunset. (If you are inclined to be angry or short-tempered, though, be very cautious about becoming too warm.) Engaging in any physical movement awakens and recharges your body, especially first thing in the morning. Try some form of intentional movement like t'ai chi, yoga, or Pilates, preferably outside. Gardening is another wonderful antidote to a frantic, fast-paced routine. Anything that allows you to slow down and become acquainted with who you are and what you really feel is key.

CHAPTER FOUR

What Will It Take to Be Loved?

One fine summer day I ran into the house with a bunch of wildflowers in my hand, like bright confetti. I had picked every flower especially for Mother. She looked down at the array of blossoms spilling out of my hand, grabbed them roughly, and tossed them aside with a look of scorn. I looked at her, baffled that she was so angry with me. I'd felt so certain the flowers would make her smile. Her eyes, like fire, scorched the soft, fragile tissue of my heart. I shrank away from her. She turned toward my brother and smiled—her love for him shimmering like a million halos of golden light.

Mother's attention was like a sandstorm—dry and blistering. I could never take a full breath around her. What had I done to deserve being choked and obliterated in this way? She had withdrawn her love before my birth, sealed it in a stone envelope, and vowed never to send it. There was nothing I could do about it.

By the time I was seven years old, I had crafted a steely shield around my heart to protect myself from the icy blade of her stare. Her resentment was tangible and yet too terrible to accept. To admit that my mother did not love me would have crushed my spirit completely. Instead, I made a pact with myself and secretly promised my heart, *I will never let that pain in. I will never let that in.* I could not have survived the truth at that young age. Mothers *always* love their children, don't they? This was a basic inviolable law of nature. I willed myself to believe that, surely, Mother loved me too.

Over time, though, I had simply written off my mother. I cancelled my membership in the Mother-Loves-Me Club. Only after many years and a tremendous amount of inner work did I allow myself to know fully and feel the truth about that crucial life-shaping relationship. I was over 30 years old before I began to accept the unthinkable: my mother truly did not care about me. I eventually understood that I was brokenhearted. By then, my heart had been shut down for years.

Many years later, I am still healing that first heartbreak. Maternal love is primal and literally determines our very heartbeat. Our initial connection to life comes solely through the mother. She is the one who provides assurance of survival—or not. She is the one who transmits and confers our most basic right to be loved and to give love—or not.

I always had much more success in relationships with men than with women. Mirroring my experience with my mother, women never seemed to like me. When I was finally able to open my heart to other women, I ventured into brand new territory—cultivating friendships with women who supported me in many ways. I learned from them that my mother did not love me because she was incapable of loving me. Mother could only love, approve of, and appreciate me to the degree that she could love, approve of, and appreciate herself. She was not capable of that because she did not love the feminine part of herself.

I'm still not "all better." The truth is that healing is a process, and while some wounds heal quickly, others take a much longer time.

THE FOURTH ENERGY CENTER: THE HEART CHAKRA

Located in the center of the chest, the fourth chakra rules over the lungs, heart, pericardium, thymus, upper back and ribs, arms, and hands. The heart is the bridge between the three lower chakras that connect us to the earth and the three upper chakras that connect us to the Infinite. Here is formed the link between the physical and the nonphysical and the bonds between self and other(s). The heart is the central organ of life that feeds the body. Key themes of this center include: giving and receiving, unconditional love, gratitude, and the willingness to be vulnerable and open. When the heart center is in balance, we are content and feel at peace; we are caring, compassionate, and forgiving.

Conditions of a distorted fourth energy center can include:

- Congestive heart failure, heart attack, mitral valve prolapse, chest pain
- Arteriosclerosis, peripheral vascular insufficiency
- Asthma, shortness of breath
- Allergies
- Lung cancer, pneumonia, bronchitis, emphysema
- Breast cancer and breast disorders, such as mastitis or cysts
- Immune system deficiencies
- Circulation problems
- Tension or pain between the shoulder blades
- Shoulder, arm, and hand issues, such as carpal tunnel

When our heart centers are out of balance, we feel it. Imbalance might begin with heartbreak, a break in our connection to our own hearts. Heartbreak is universal. Does any human being make it through life without experiencing heartbreak at least once? Heartbreak at an early age may be caused by rejection or betrayal from a parent, friend, teacher, or a "first love." Later, love can break our hearts in a hundred different ways. Someone may leave us or die. Heartbreak can occur over a loss of trust in someone or something we deeply believed in.

What we do with our feelings in times of heartbreak is key. Many of us have modeled our reactions on what our parents advised us as children. They may have told us not to cry when a favorite friend moved away or insisted we "wipe our tears and be a big girl" when a school crush did not return our affections. Later on, we may have been told to "buck up and get over it" when we didn't make the swim team, get asked to the prom, or get into the university of our choice.

Shutting down the heart is a common response when pain seems unbearable. But a heart that is shut down from the bad stuff—the feelings we don't want to feel—also becomes closed off from the good stuff, the love we most want to receive. When we shut down our hearts, we diminish our capacity not only to give and receive love, but also to remain healthy.

A CLOSED AND BROKEN HEART

The heart is the central organ in the body, the life giver. A heart that is closed to minimize pain can become the catalyst for illness. Many people who show up in my office with angina, arteriosclerosis, or other conditions related to the fourth chakra have unknowingly shut down their hearts to protect themselves. They may not remember when or how they shut down, but the price they pay is high.

Often, homosexuals shut down their hearts at an early age so as not to feel the rejection of family and friends who oppose their sexual orientation. HIV is an immune deficiency disorder involving the thymus gland, which sits above the heart and behind the sternum. The thymus helps the body fight disease by producing hormones that aid in the production of T-cells, vital players in healthy immune system functioning.

The thymus may become diseased when a battle wages inside the self. A lack of self-love or self-acceptance—a feeling of being unlovable for who we are or a feeling that we have to fight to be loved as we are—can create an environment of ill health inside the body. Anything that restricts or blocks the flow of energy to the body will result in illness. Suppressed emotions such as anger or shame contribute to the creation of a weakened immune system. Emotions *can kill* if suppressed.

A disorder that is common to this chakra is lung cancer, which caused the death of Dana Reeve, wife of the late actor Christopher Reeve, fondly remembered as "Superman." She was diagnosed with lung cancer shortly after her husband's death. A nonsmoker, Dana died not long after her husband, leaving a 13-year-old son without either parent. The deep wells of suppressed grief that she had carried in her lungs as far back as her husband's paralyzing horseback accident were possibly unleashed with her husband's passing.

Grief is messy and painful. We often mask it with anger. Some of us are terrified that giving in to our sorrow means we will get trapped in it, never to recover. But grieving is necessary when we encounter a loss. To grieve is to allow ourselves to be with our sadness, to feel it and let it wash over us. If we don't grieve, if we push our feelings down, they may emerge later as illness.

Breast cancer is also clearly related to the heart chakra. Multi-platinum rock singer/songwriter and musician Melissa Etheridge became the public face of breast cancer when she appeared at the 2005 Grammy Awards, bald from chemotherapy, and turned her performance of Janis Joplin's "Piece of My Heart" into the highlight of the evening. A brave lady, Etheridge had come out as a lesbian at the Triangle Ball in 1993 for President Bill Clinton's first inauguration.

She has had her share of heartbreak. In her memoir, *The Truth Is . . . My Life in Love and Music,* Etheridge reveals the dark secret of her childhood: she was molested by her older sister for over five years, starting when she was a child of six. In the book, she also talked about the pain of her upbringing, her childhood isolation, and depression. Writing about the abuse and her broken heart from the end of her relationship with Julie Cypher, mother of their two children (by sperm donor rock legend David Crosby) helped her to move forward with her life. Since then, she has had a commitment ceremony celebrating her partnership with actress Tammy Lynn Michaels, who gave birth to their twins in 2006.

As Etheridge said in an interview on CNN, "I learned very early on that I could write truths, I could write about sadness or anger, where I couldn't actually speak it." While her early songs were filled with sadness, a fear of abandonment, and a painful cry for love, her more recent work is upbeat, reflecting the hard-won peace of her heart.

TAKING PERSONAL INVENTORY

As I healed from an upbringing that almost destroyed my ability to love, I realized that I had to develop a new capacity. I began to explore the strength of my heart by unabashedly exposing it to the changes and growth playing out in my life. I regularly "took inventory" of my heart chakra to stay conscious about remaining open to loving and being loved.

If you are not attracting love into your life, you might ask yourself if your heart is truly open to love or if you are harboring and feeding old hurts. Taking personal inventory is a powerful way to see if your heart is open or closed.

Sit quietly with yourself and ask:

- What am I feeling?
- Where am I hurting?
- How am I holding love back?
- Why am I withholding love?
- Could I be more loving to others and myself?
- Do I think I need to be perfect to be loved?
- How could I love myself just as I am?
- What does self-acceptance look like to me?
- Have I isolated myself from others?
- Do I lack empathy or am I afraid of intimacy?
- Am I excessively drawn to others, in need of their approval and their love?
- Am I co-dependent, giving too much attention to the needs of others and not enough to my own?
- Am I enough now? If not, when will I be enough?

These explorations can help us evaluate imbalances in the fourth energy center. As we come to know ourselves better, the answers to these questions can help us know when, where, and how our hearts need healing.

Real love is an emotion of truth. Love has the power to heal all the wounds we may have suffered—if we allow it to flow.

My own life was blessed by the arrival of my husband. I think my mother knew instinctively when I met Eric that I had found true love, and she resented me for it. When Eric announced our engagement at a party, my mother spoke to me through gritted teeth and warned, "You will not marry that French mountain climber!" But I did marry him—a gentle, loving man who manifested the best qualities of my father.

I had the wisdom to recognize Eric's love and the willingness to receive it. Eric and I have had our struggles, to be sure. But he has been a remarkable source of strength, loving me through some of the most painful times of my life—when I was manic depressive, acting out sexually with a string of men in my 20s, drinking, and generally living out of control. Eventually, I came to believe in and trust his love.

FORGIVENESS

When I closed my heart as a child to protect myself from my mother, it set up a domino effect that took years to reverse. My shoulders rounded to protect the front of my heart and my heart collapsed inside my rib cage. I had closed down the front of my heart because loving wasn't safe. I could not express love or my feelings and desires in a direct way.

My learned pattern of survival is common to people who have been wounded in the heart. I see this pattern frequently in clients who have experienced infidelity. Their partners have cheated, and they have instinctively shut down their hearts. The rear part of their hearts either deflates into helplessness, causing them to become powerless victims, or it inflates and they become determined and intractable.

Becky, a 50-year-old woman, came to my office with a diagnosis of hardening of the arteries. Ten years previously, Becky's husband had an affair. When she discovered his infidelity, she closed down and promised herself, "I will *never* forgive him." It became her anthem over the years, a hundred-percent commitment to bitterness and hard-heartedness. She

Checking In

Ask yourself, how am I feeling now?
What (who) caused these feelings?
When (where, why) did these feelings arise?
Can I be with these feelings without
denying or judging them?

readily and rather proudly admitted her position, but she was unconscious of the havoc it was causing in her body and oblivious to the pain this was causing her children.

Becky's refusal to forgive her husband became like a brick wall around her heart. In turn, her arteries—the conduits of blood and life—became hard and thickened with rage. I could tell that it would be difficult to reach her. She was set in her position, convinced she was right, even though her angry stance made her unhappy. I could see that if she did not ease up on her anger and begin to forgive her husband, she would continue courting a heart attack.

Hardening is just what it sounds like—a constriction of energy. The flow of energy in the body, specifically to the heart, becomes restricted, as does the amount of love energy that can flow into us and out to others. This doesn't feel good to the person who is hardening—holding back—nor does it feel good to anyone else in their sphere.

Initially, Becky was immovable. She wanted me to "fix her," but she wanted nothing to do with whatever I suggested. She did not want to hear that she could do something, especially if it involved changing her mind about her husband. "I have every right to be angry," she said when I told her that the anger could ultimately destroy her health. As gently as I could, I asked her to consider the possibility of forgiving him, if only to improve her health. Slowly but surely, Becky began to recognize the connection between the onset of her disease and the vow she made to never forgive.

Her real awakening happened when our discussion turned to her childhood. She remembered that she made the same vow as a child of ten when her father walked out the door, never to return. The synchronicity was interesting. She was ten when her father left and it was in her tenth year of marriage that her husband had his affair. As I scanned her field, I saw scenes that I shared with her. I suggested that she might not know all the reasons her father had left. Resistant to that possibility, she claimed to know everything. I asked her if she had told her own young children everything when she and her husband fought or had arguments.

No, she acknowledged, she did not tell the children the whole truth. I asked if it was possible that her mother did not tell her the whole truth. "Yes," she finally admitted, "it is possible."

I asked her to visualize the last day she had seen her father and to feel again the emotions she had denied herself at the time. In doing so, she wept very old tears, cleansing the emotions from her body. At the close of this session, Becky made a connection that opened the door to her healing, "I never cried after my father left. I thought if I was a big girl like my mother asked me to be, Daddy would come back. He never did, and he never called. I never forgave him, but I told everybody I was okay. I never believed that anybody would ever really love me. I guess I expected my husband to hurt me."

As she softened and realized she was projecting her anger at her father onto her husband, she actually began to feel more loving and was able to begin to forgive her husband. She acknowledged that from the beginning she had believed that her husband would eventually leave. She'd always been waiting for the other shoe to drop, just as it had with her father. Becky realized that she had acted out her mother's script—pushing her husband away with her unrelenting anger and lack of trust.

When Becky began to trust and forgive, the condition of her arteries improved. She continues to get better as she becomes more conscious of her struggle with bitterness.

MAKING THE CONNECTION

Often the energetic pattern of an illness is unleashed as a result of crisis or trauma. Initially, most clients have difficulty believing that unexpressed emotions can lead to disease, yet when they make the connections between their own stories and their illnesses, the light of awareness comes on. This was true with Claudia.

Claudia was in a new marriage and secretly did not want children. Her husband wanted a child and told her that she could maintain her career and have a family. But Claudia had seen other women in her field attempt the dual role and believed it to be an impossible feat. The life of a broadcast journalist was unpredictable by definition, and she had no desire to sacrifice her mobility and independence to motherhood. Nor could she envision adjusting the lifestyle she and her husband currently enjoyed, the ski trips and tropical vacations, several homes, and a busy social life. Although they could easily afford a nanny, Claudia liked their jet-set life and did not really want to interrupt it for a child. But she also did not want to risk losing her husband.

At the age of 40, Claudia went along with her husband's wish and became pregnant. She dropped down to part-time work, and then quit entirely after the baby was born. Claudia developed painful mastitis (inflammation in the breasts) and could not nurse her newborn. When she came to see me, her daughter was in nursery school, but Claudia had not returned to work. She had suffered from chronic mastitis for several years and felt desperate. When I suggested she might have some negative feelings about being a stay-at-home mom rather than a career woman, she grew defensive. She was unwilling to consider the possibility that she harbored regret or resentment or that it could be connected to her breast infection. Although Claudia was in tune with and commit-ted to her personal growth, this was her blind spot.

Often our emotional blind spots have to do with our "wiring" around basic survival issues. In Claudia's case, she felt that her marriage depended on having a child—and being truthful about not wanting a child could have destroyed the marriage.

Women are frequently at war with themselves about motherhood and careers. We are supposed to do every-thing—have careers, run families, be there for our partners, hold it all together, and be beautiful. It's an impossible fan-tasy. We cannot do it all. Those of us who still believe we can are often like bombs set to explode. Claudia was a time bomb, especially since she could not admit what she truly felt.

Claudia's opening in awareness happened on her second visit. When I suggested she might get a part-time job now that her daughter was older, she snapped at me angrily, "You expect me to have a life I love . . . and a child?" Her own words stopped her dead in her tracks. She looked at me in stunned silence. "You think I might be angry that I had to give up my career for my daughter? I swore I wouldn't become my mother, who slammed kitchen cupboards and told me I was the reason her life was so boring."

Making the connection between her misery and motherhood was pivotal for Claudia. Realizing that she had been unconsciously blaming her daughter for the loss of her career allowed her to reconsider her core beliefs and reorder her priorities.

After a number of sessions to help Claudia clear her breast area of the residue of old emotions, her infection began to diminish. She is now working again and loving it. Her daughter goes to after-school dance classes while Claudia works. Mother, daughter, and husband are all thriving. As Claudia found out, we cannot lie to ourselves—the lies manifest in our bodies or in our relationships. What we try to hide hurts us. The truth heals us.

HEART ATTACK!

Heart attacks can be extreme manifestations of a lack of love. From the perspective of energy medicine, heart disease can be a physical expression of either a lack or the loss of love. From my point of view, former President Bill Clinton is a powerful example of someone who suffered a broken heart that manifested on the physical level as disease. Clinton's sexual indiscretion with Monica Lewinsky and the public investigation that followed caused him intense shame and a loss of respect in the eyes of the American people. His fall from grace was undeniable, and his heart bore the brunt of that emotional pain.

In 2004, when the former president entered the hospital complaining of chest pains, doctors found all three major arteries severely blocked. After undergoing bypass surgery, he looked like a man who had been emotionally disemboweled. And I would assert that he was. Violating the integrity of his marriage and losing the respect, admiration, and love of the world, which had fed his soul so deeply during his administration, took a heavy toll on his heart. Although Clinton blamed his heart damage on eating too much fast food during his presidency, there may well have been an emotional cause.

Any illness, even a heart attack, can be a gift in disguise. It can serve to open and soften us. Coming close to death often awakens an appreciation and a longing for closeness with the people we love. Many people, when they learn that they are dying or have a near-death experience, rush to their loved ones and say, "I love you, I love you, I love you." Love is the most powerful force on earth. Awakening the love in our own hearts can heal us.

The potential always exists for illness to cause change for the good. It happened to my mother. Although I rarely attended family events, one year I sensed that my mother was not well and that I should join the family for Thanksgiving. Mother had a gift for creating picture-perfect Thanksgiving Day dinners. After dinner, Mother seemed fine, and I thought to myself that my intuition had been inaccurate. But shortly after I left, I received an urgent call: Mother had been rushed to the hospital with a heart attack. After her recovery, everyone in the family commented on how much softer my mother seemed. It was as if the attack had thawed her heart. In a stunning transformation, she was gentler and more loving to everyone—even me. For the first time I experienced the grace of her caring and tender self.

Thank God It's Monday!

Monday mornings are classic times for heart attacks.
Studies show that more people experience heart attacks
between 8 a.m. and 9 a.m. on Monday mornings,
the start of their workweek, than at any other time.
When you do what you love, you
will genuinely welcome Monday mornings.

We are all composed of both the dark and the light. Our primary expression of either dark or light can shift at any time when a transformational catalyst is present. In my mother's case, a heart attack was just such a catalytic event.

For many people, direct encounters with mortality "flip the switch" and allow their light to shine through. The award-winning television host, Larry King, is a prime example of someone whose life has been altered by heart attacks. The first to affect him was his father's, who died at the age of 44 from a heart attack when King was nine years old. His mother had to go on welfare, and after high school he was unable to go to college because he had to help support her.

Perhaps this painful past triggered his tendency toward major denial. Despite smoking three packs of cigarettes a day, he believed he was immortal. Then, when he was interviewing Dr. C. Everett Koop, the Surgeon General, Dr. Koop asked him if he felt all right. Sure, he said. Dr. Koop said, "Well, you don't look good." That night King woke up with terrible pain in his right arm and shoulder. After an hour waiting in the hospital emergency room, his pain eased and he tried to leave, but his driver was circling the block and an ER attendant brought King back. He was admitted and later had to undergo triple bypass surgery. He stopped smoking that day.

Since then, King has been noted for his humanitarian and charitable work in heart disease, including the establishment of the Larry King Cardiac Foundation. He has written two books about living with heart disease and speaks about how the heart attack and bypass surgery changed his life. He has also given $1 million to George Washington University's School of Media and Public Affairs for scholarships to students from disadvantaged backgrounds.

A BALANCED FOURTH CHAKRA

None of us are all dark or light, and miraculous changes can and do occur when circumstances allow our hidden face to come forward. Tremendous healing can occur at such times; the pain of a lifetime can be erased in a single moment of pure forgiveness. Unconditional love, forgiveness, and surrender—the ability to "let go and let God"—are the hallmarks of a heart chakra in perfect balance. These abilities are not easily achieved in the face of what would otherwise cause reactions of anger or fear.

When someone in our midst extends compassion and forgiveness when anger would have been easier, all of us are elevated. The case of the Amish parents who forgave their daughters' killer is a perfect demonstration of this. In October of 2006, a mentally-disturbed milk truck driver stormed into the one-room schoolhouse in Nickel Mines, PA, and shot ten young girls, five of whom died. The world watched in amazement as the Amish families extended forgiveness toward the killer and his family, with some of those who had lost children even attending the killer's burial service.

A year after the tragic event, the Amish community donated money to the killer's widow and her three young children. This doesn't mean that the Amish didn't suffer. Many of those involved have received therapy, some of the children are dealing with "emotional instabilities," and the boys (who were released from the school before the killer shot the girls) are dealing with survivor's guilt and still have nightmares. But none of that has changed the Amish commitment to forgive and help others.

Unconditional love is an act of an open heart, an act of the divine coursing through our veins. Ordinary people can and do demonstrate it.

Many people love broadly and fully and have lives of utmost compassion, not only personally but also on public and even global scales. An example of someone with an integrated heart chakra is Montel Williams, who hosted *The Montel Williams Show,* a nationally syndicated program that often centered on reuniting families torn apart by different circumstances—by drugs, racism, unfaithfulness, etc. He is a man who is not afraid of his heart, a man who feels deeply and shows it. He approached the guests on his show in a true heart-to-heart fashion and chose the content of his show based on his own life experiences.

Born in a Baltimore ghetto, Williams is a decorated naval intelligence officer who spent 22 years in the Navy, a renowned motivational speaker, an author of numerous books all aimed at helping others, and a dedicated philanthropist. The Navy presented Williams with its Superior Public Service Award for his continuous support and recognition of sailors, Marines, and their families throughout the 17 years of his television show, which ended in May 2008.

When Williams was diagnosed with multiple sclerosis in 1999, he learned there was no cure. He realized he had a choice: to see himself as the victim of a terrible disease or to use his illness as a way to make a difference in the lives of the millions who suffer from MS. He clearly chose with his heart, as he now heads the Montel Williams MS Foundation, which directs research for treatments and helps make MS drugs available to everyone. He has also become an advocate for the legalization of medical marijuana for qualified patients, as it helped considerably in relieving his own pain.

Healing our hearts and our fourth energy centers takes consciousness. We all need to set aside time to do the work of self-healing. Meditation and journaling are important for consciously approaching this work. Greg Louganis, the back-to-back winning Olympic medalist regarded as the greatest competitive diver of all time, was diagnosed as HIV positive in 1988 as he trained for the Seoul Games. Advised not to reveal his diagnosis, it was during these Olympics that he hit his head on the diving board and agonized over whether or not the light bleeding had posed a danger of infection to fellow competitors (it did not). He used journaling as a way to get through this difficult time.

About his writing he said, "It was really sad stuff. But it was something that I needed to get out. When I was growing up, I could understand how somebody could die of sadness.

They didn't kill themselves; they just died of sadness. So those were the feelings that I was dealing with." Later, psychotherapy and antidepressant medication also helped, as did the 1995 publication of his autobiography, *Breaking the Surface,* where he announced his HIV status as well as revealing the domestic abuse and rape he had suffered from a live-in gay lover (he then lost all his corporate sponsors, with the exception of Speedo). He learned how to talk publicly and openly about issues such as depression, dyslexia, and being HIV-positive, and is now able to help many others.

Combining the following checklist with the Personal Inventory questions on page 90 will give you a very clear and accurate picture of your heart space.

CHECKLIST

To determine the state of your fourth energy center, focus on the following questions:

1. Do I have any of the conditions listed on page 86?
2. Have I ever felt betrayed by a love partner? What did I do as a result?
3. Have I been diagnosed with heart-related problems or lung disease?
4. Do my hands or arms ache?
5. Do I suffer from emphysema or recurring bouts of pneumonia?
6. Have I ever felt rejected by family or friends? What did I do with my pain?

7. Is love scary to me? Or do I give and receive it easily?
8. Have I been told that I criticize and judge people?
9. Have I forgiven myself or others for past infractions, or do I still harbor resentment?
10. Which attributes could I develop more—altruism, love, compassion, forgiveness, hope, trust, harmony, support?

Loving and being loved is our right. Health and vigor are the natural results of balanced energy systems. Rich and balanced relationships function in the flow of giving and receiving. Faced with any imbalance, listen to your body, mind, and heart, and do what works. Do what you love, and it will reward you in kind. Be open to loving yourself and others more. Seek to soften the rigid walls you have erected around your heart. Dig out the roots of your consciousness where you buried any hope of experiencing real love. One of the best ways to open a closed heart is through giving and receiving love with a pet—a dog, cat, horse, or even a bird can help heal earlier heartbreak and teach us how to love again. Pets love us unconditionally and make it safe for us to learn to love again.

CHAPTER FIVE

Thou Shalt Speak Your Truth

When I was seven, I sat in the cool interior of the church waiting to make my first confession and wondering if Father Fitzgerald would recognize my voice. A devout and obedient child, I was a familiar face to the priest. "Bless me, Father, for I have sinned," I began as instructed after entering the confessional. "This is my First Confession." How do I confess a mortal sin when I didn't even know its name? How could I explain that no matter how hard I tried, I could not make Mother smile? I began with simple "venial" sins: "I teased my brother; I chased the dog."

Father Fitzgerald asked, "Did you obey your parents?" In little whispers I told him I had tried, but no matter how well I behaved, Mother was always unhappy with me. "How dare you criticize your parents!" thundered from his side of the screen. "You have disobeyed the Fourth Commandment: Honor thy Mother and thy Father." He then gave me a penance of three Hail Marys and sent me out of the confessional hissing beneath his breath, "I will devise a special penance for such a wicked girl."

I left the confessional box, terrified. Mother was waiting, but I dared not speak to her about what had just happened. Consumed by a cloud of guilt for being such a bad child, I crept into the pew to say my penance.

We were the perfect family, starched and pressed and polished to a fine gleam. Except the whole thing was a lie. Bad Daddy was making regular forays into my bedroom. Years later when I confronted my mother about the abuse, she said, "We don't talk about those kinds of things in our family." Mother wore the high-priced fashion label Deny & Pretend. THOU SHALT NOT SPEAK YOUR TRUTH was etched into the welcome mat outside our front door.

Living lies makes us crazy. We feel one way and pretend to feel another. We experience something and act like it isn't happening. I was a master at living this split and keeping my feelings bottled up. I didn't consciously know that I was suppressing the truth. I just knew that I was forbidden to say anything about what troubled me and thus assumed I was the "problem," as all children do.

Mother did not tolerate anger in any form. If I said anything out of turn, she washed my mouth out with soap. Tears were off-limits; no stain could fall on the carefully drawn picture of our perfect life.

I don't remember ever asking for something I really wanted or expressing who I was. I was terrified of displeasing Mother. By the time I was five I had learned to toe the line. Mother told me repeatedly who I was to be and tyrannized me into denying the truth. It seemed I was always forced to shut my mouth, except on those unspeakable occasions when my father forced my mouth open. The lie I lived became the lie I gave to the world.

For my father, the culture we called *home* included being humiliated and ridiculed by my mother at the dinner table many nights. He meekly endured it, like a good soldier. She controlled what he ate, what he wore, and how he spent every penny he made. Only rarely, perhaps once a year, when my father couldn't take Mother's relentless bullying anymore, he would blow his top. His roar on such occasions sent all of us scurrying. Otherwise, he choked down his frustration, never speaking his truth, just as he had never spoken his truth as a child.

When wrongs are hushed, we learn that we have no choice but to silence our voices. Where does the truth go when it's not expressed? We may lie to survive, but the body cannot; it never lies. The lies I kept within me as a child expressed themselves as chronic tonsillitis at five and six, teeth grinding at seven, an "accidental fall" at nine, and distorted and wounded digestive organs and female reproductive parts at twelve and thirteen. Later on, the lies became promiscuity, manic depression, alcohol and drug abuse, heart arrhythmia, metabolic disorders, and cancer. Rage and sorrow strangled my larynx, creating so much tension that I often had a very real "pain in the neck." My body had become a literal expression of the pain I couldn't speak or express any other way.

FAKING A LIFE

When we silence what's wrong, we also silence what's right. It took me a long time—and a serious illness—to begin expressing the truth of what I had experienced and finally the truth of my creative self. I had learned to force my will on the world and have the will of others forced on me. Never had I imagined that life could be lived through a flow of God-given gifts, creatively expressed.

My true voice went underground until age fifteen when Cindy—my rebellious side—stepped up to the plate and all hell broke loose. At this time, she embodied the suppressed, perverted truth that burst out of its tight little wrapping and was voiced in seductive ways. But this expression wasn't the *honest* truth; Cindy was merely expressing pain. In manic phases, I tore around town and acted out in increasingly sexual and obnoxious ways as the pain spoke the only language it knew. That part of me had a mouth and was out to shock. Because I lived in shock, I had no other choice. When so much pain has been suppressed for so long, it comes out with a sting and a stench. What I had no ability to feel or express—not as a child, not for a very long time—was my vulnerability. The true me— the soft, frightened, curious, still-in-discovery, gentle, uncertain, insecure parts of myself—was nowhere to be found.

For many years, my voice was unequivocally stifled. I put on a facade of perfection to mask every feature of my personal self and forced myself to seem happy when I was not. I acted as if I had no feelings when I had plenty and projected an image of certainty and perfection at all times.

At age eighteen, I had high ambitions and told my parents that I wanted to go to Sarah Lawrence College and study the arts. Writing, music, and dance seemed to be the keys for unlocking who I really was. But my mother would hear nothing of that: I was to attend a Jesuit college close to home so she could continue to control me. After college, I went straight to law school. On my first day, I entered the multi-tiered amphitheater and sat in the very last row out of fear that someone might look at me.

Along with fear, I carried the burden of shame and embarrassment. In a profession where public speaking is essential, I was afflicted with an overwhelming fear of it. When I was first out of law school and representing a client in a jury trial, I went to lunch with a colleague. Noticing my nervousness, he said, "Have a drink, take the edge off." Oh, he was so right! I quickly got to the point where I didn't just take the edge off, I took the whole table off! I stepped up my drinking and Valium use to handle my dread of being revealed as a fraud. I faked my whole life, pretending to be happy when I was scared, angry, hurt, or devastated.

At work, I employed a seductive routine that helped me make it through the day. I was good and successful at the practice of law. Although I was a stickler for the truth with my clients, I continued to lie through my teeth about myself. I lived the lie of a hard-drinking, hard-driving, sexually free young woman. I projected *liberation* in every sense of the word, choosing multiple sexual partners, handling my financial investments, and building a legal career that had no glass ceiling. In any meeting with a room full of men, I led with my sexuality. I cultivated a string of male conquests, one after the other like pearls in a necklace. This was the part of me that needed the kind of approval I had always gotten from Daddy.

Ironically, although I seemed to be in charge—a woman who knew her own mind and wasn't afraid to speak it—nothing could have been further from the truth. My public persona belied a girl who was vulnerable, lost, and in total fear of being found out, of not measuring up, of being rejected. I drank or took drugs and did extreme sports. I made every effort to hide an inadequate self, first from myself and then from the rest of the world.

My drinking led to blackouts. I found myself waking up in a stranger's bed not knowing what had happened or how I'd gotten there. The truth is anathema to an active alcoholic. The truth of how I really felt and who I really was began to surface

Find Your Voice . . . Speak Your Choice

When you are used to going with the flow
so as not to rock the boat, never voicing
what you really want and how you feel,
it is a challenge to start speaking the truth.
Next time you are asked something, stop and ask yourself,
what do I really want?
When you answer truthfully, you honor yourself
and give others permission to honor themselves too.

when Eric spoke my name and the word *alcoholic* in the same sentence. That was the beginning of the end of the lies.

I went to my first Alcoholics Anonymous meeting the next morning, dressed to kill and wearing a pair of $1,800 cowboy boots. What I didn't realize is that "newcomers" often show up for their first meetings looking totally together but with a life that's in shambles just beneath the surface. I was extraordinarily impressed with AA; people were being so *alarmingly honest.* They were speaking the *real* truth and laying it all out there without artifice. I had never told the truth in my entire life. *Never.* And the more alcohol I poured down my throat, the less worried I was about the lies that came out. It took years before I could start telling the truth. I quit drinking far more easily than I stopped lying.

THE FIFTH ENERGY CENTER: THE THROAT CHAKRA

The fifth energy center, located at the throat, is primarily associated with creative expression. Its key theme is *speaking the truth*—expressing who we are, what we feel, and what we believe—whether through verbal or nonverbal communication. Sound comes through the throat and enables expression through spoken words and the songs we sing. The "messengers" of the fifth energy center are *voice* and *choice.* We manifest how we live, what we wear, what we eat, and even what our dreams are by giving them voice. Choice gives voice to our desires, and, in turn, our voice expresses our choice.

The fifth chakra is connected to the throat, neck, shoulders, mouth, jaw, and teeth, as well as to the nasal sinuses, vocal chords, trachea and esophagus, cervical vertebrae, and ears. The thyroid, parathyroid, and the hypothalamus, which control the autonomic nervous system, are also located here.

When this area is out of balance, the following conditions can arise:

- TMJ (temporomandibular joint) disorder in the jaw
- Swollen glands in the throat, throat cancer
- Neck problems
- Chronic childhood tonsillitis
- Hypo- and hyperthyroidism, thyroiditis, thyroid cancer, Hashimoto's, Grave's disease
- Chronic sinus problems
- Any disorders of the throat, voice, mouth, teeth, or gums

Thyroid conditions typically arise after physical or emotional crises. The butterfly-shaped thyroid gland that sits in the front of the neck regulates the body's metabolism. Synthetic thyroid—the primary solution allopathic medicine turns to for thyroid deficiency—is among the top three most frequently prescribed drugs in the United States. But this "Band-Aid" approach fails to address the underlying cause. It is no coincidence, given the cultural suppression of women, that thyroid conditions are more prevalent in women than men by a ratio of five to one.

The throat is designed to keep itself clear by discharging excess energy through speech or the emission of sound.

Sometimes it's necessary to take it up a notch and even yell or scream to clear this center. The throat chakra functions as a regulator, controlling what we let out or keep in. It is also the seat of subtle guidance, providing us with a quiet voice from within that guides us in every situation—if we take the time to listen. Unfortunately, when we experience conflict between our head and our heart, we can shut down that "still small voice" within. We may refuse to listen to our inner guidance or to those around us. This dynamic shuts down the normal processes of this center.

When the throat area has distortions, issues can develop. These may include an inability to communicate effectively, an unwillingness to hear or act on guidance, or a sense of having lost the rhythm of life. Other manifestations can include an inability to receive what is given by others, a tendency to blame others for our experiences, or an urge to force things to happen. People who are out of balance in this area may talk too much or speak in inappropriate ways. They may gossip, stutter, or have difficulty being quiet. Sometimes they are too loud. They may find it hard to put words together or have a fear of speaking, or they may be secretive, excessively shy, or tone deaf.

Throughout the generations, women have consistently lost their identities and stopped living their truth when they marry. And men and women have both denied the truth for the sake of their careers.

Looking at Rock Hudson's life, we see that he denied his homosexuality and AIDS until right before his death. The

Hollywood star system was a force to be reckoned with at the start of the 1950s, when tall, dark, and handsome Hudson started out. A star of romantic light comedies along with Doris Day, the leading man—a symbol of the charming and glamorous playboy—was virtually a prisoner of a system that could not and would not allow him to acknowledge his real self. But when he sought treatment in Paris, the rumors that he was suffering from AIDS were confirmed. Photographs showed the once vital man to be gaunt and unrecognizable. His death in 1985 focused world attention on the AIDS virus. He became "the face of AIDS," helping to bring the hush-hush topic out in the open. Shortly before his death, when the truth was finally out, Hudson said, "I am not happy I am sick. I am not happy I have AIDS. But if that is helping others, I can at least know my own misfortune has had some positive worth."

His story is a common one that illustrates the cost of repressing our truth or not asking for what we need, of living in accordance with someone else's wants—whether real or imagined. What this ultimately costs us is our happiness, our sense of connection with ourselves, our relationships with those we love, our health, and sometimes our very lives.

IN PARTNERSHIP WITH TRUTH

In this country, we pride ourselves on freedom of speech and often are critical of cultures that restrict free expression. But what happens when we ourselves squelch our own right to free expression? When we are our own tyrant and jailer?

Kelly came into my office with metastasized thyroid cancer. She had undergone surgery to remove the thyroid gland the year before, but the cancer had recurred in adjacent cervical vertebrae. Looking deeply in Kelly's energy field, I saw distortions in her fifth chakra that were caused by the lies she forced herself to live.

Kelly had been in a long-term lesbian relationship, but she was not "out." In the company of heterosexual clients, she pretended to be straight. Though gifted landscape designers, she and her girlfriend had not made much money in the landscaping business they started together. Life was hard, and Kelly was tired of being poor. A successful young attorney hired her to design the gardens on his property. When he fell in love with Kelly and asked her to marry him, she accepted his proposal and left her lesbian lover. Kelly's decision was a choice of will rather than a choice of the heart. Her new husband was fun, warm, and loving, and she convinced herself that her lesbianism had been no more than a passing phase.

Even when Kelly became really sick, she wasn't ready to be honest. She was ashamed of her love of women and unwilling to acknowledge it as an authentic expression of who she really was. Although part of her desperately wanted help, another part insisted on maintaining her facade, thus keeping her illness intact. Like her mother often said, Kelly felt she had "made her bed and had to lie in it."

We cannot thrive unless we are true to ourselves. Maintaining relationships that don't nourish us diminishes our ability to flourish emotionally, physically, and even financially. Though she had only occasional contact with her ex-lover, Kelly insisted that she was entirely happy with her husband. She shrugged off her gay experiences as nothing more than youthful experimentation. The last time I saw Kelly, she was scheduled for another surgery, but her physicians were not hopeful.

When we are paralyzed by fear—horrified of the consequences that revealing the truth might bring—we go to great lengths to foster the lie. We protect and nurture the lie, ignoring the cost to our personal integrity. Facing our truth allows us to live the life we are meant to live.

SPEAKING UP

No relationship is easy. Good ones take work and the willingness to express our truth. Jim, in his early 50s, initially came to see me in the hope of avoiding jaw surgery for severe TMJ dysfunction, a common condition characterized by extreme pain in the jaw and surrounding tissues. My first observation was striking: I immediately saw that his jaw was impacted by his relationship with his wife. He confided right off the bat that his overly sensitive wife misunderstood him. Although he admitted that he had a tendency to "put his foot in his mouth" and say the wrong things, he firmly believed she just didn't understand him and even doubted that she really loved him. From his wife's viewpoint, Jim was sloppy in his communications and unable to give or receive love. His wife was becoming more and more upset as of late, but Jim blamed it on "the damn cell phone." Not one to keep his phone on hand, Jim was often out of range when it rang. He hated feeling like he was "on a leash," but his wife insisted on being able to reach him when she needed him; this issue between them often erupted into a fight.

As we began to dig deeper into the control issue, Jim shared that his father had ridiculed his heart's desire to pursue music. He was the lead singer of a garage band in high school and was accepted into a music conservatory, but his father insisted a career in music would only lead to Jim becoming a lounge singer at the Ramada Inn. Jim's father had worked the line at General Motors and moved up to management. He was making a good living and wanted his son to do the same. When Jim's high school girlfriend got pregnant, he felt his fate was sealed. Seeing no other choice, he got married and joined his father at GM. He eventually surpassed his father's success by working his way up to a senior executive position.

Jim and his wife began having serious problems when their young son started to exhibit musical talent. His wife encouraged their son's musical gifts and enlisted Jim to take him to his weekend singing lessons. Jim was often unavailable or begrudged the task when he was around. Frequently, he showed up late or did not communicate well with his wife, making it harder for her to rely on him.

To begin treating Jim, we cleared his fifth energy center using several energy techniques involving sound, and then I recommended that he take singing lessons with his son to keep his throat open and vital. At first he thought my suggestion preposterous, but in time he warmed to the idea. He realized this would enhance his relationship with his son and provide him with an outlet for the musical interest he had suppressed. I also suggested he practice writing his truth in a journal and express himself more directly with his wife. "I can't tell her I really want to start a garage band with a couple of guys at work, can I?" he asked me. He tried it and came back the next week elated at the result. His wife was on board if it was something that would make him happy!

Through our work together, Jim's fifth chakra opened and became more balanced. He began to see that he had hidden his deepest truths from himself and from his wife and, rather than go with the flow of the natural rhythm of life, had forced his will on the people he loved. He and his wife began couple's therapy to improve their communication. Within a year of adopting these new strategies, Jim's doctor confirmed that his painful jaw condition had improved to the extent that surgery was no longer required.

A BALANCED FIFTH CHAKRA

From an energy perspective, the throat is the power center of living from our truth. When balanced and healthy, we live from our dreams, our visions, our greater purpose, our integrity, our love of who we are, and our blessings in life.

A full, resonant quality to a person's voice, easy communication, and creative fluency indicate balance of the fifth energy center. Perhaps one of the most inspirational examples of a person with a well-integrated fifth chakra is Dr. Martin Luther King, Jr., who used his voice to change the world. King, a Baptist minister and political activist, spearheaded the American civil rights movement and, at a time when many were afraid to speak, used the full force of his speech to win support for the civil rights cause. He won the Nobel Peace Prize for his work before being assassinated in 1968. Even now, if we listen to his famous "I Have a Dream" speech, the sound of his voice resonates deeply within us.

Another example of someone with a healthy and balanced fifth energy center is actress and activist Jane Fonda, an empowered and outspoken woman who once silenced herself and allowed her voice to be silenced by the men in her life. Now in her sixties, Fonda is a woman who speaks her mind proudly and loudly. In her autobiography, *My Life So Far,* Fonda describes leaving her marriage to Ted Turner as "a divorce from patriarchy" and "symbolic of *leaving my father's house.*" The paternalistic, patriarchal, and restrictive paradigm that keeps women in a place of secondary importance behind their male family members was no longer viable for her.

Yet another celebrity with a healthy fifth energy center is actor, filmmaker, and environmental activist Robert Redford, founder of the Sundance Film Festival in Park City, Utah. He has spoken out about alternative energy sources, delivering his message through an advocacy campaign called "Kick the Oil Habit," in which he invites the American public to demand authentic leadership from politicians. Redford seems to know clearly who he is, and he feels free to take his show on the road. His ability to turn vision into action is exemplified by the Sundance Film Festival, which gives voice to independent filmmakers. *Speak the truth and create platforms to speak it far and wide* seems to be Redford's mantra—a good example for all of us to follow.

Speaking out is also a way to overcome grief. Katie Couric took an unpalatable subject, colon cancer, and brought it front and center to the vast audience in television land after her husband died of the disease in 1998. As co-host of NBC's *Today* show and as the managing editor and first solo female anchor of the *CBS Evening News* (one of the "big three" weekday nightly news broadcasts), Couric has covered breaking-news events on national and international stories. Yet she took the very

There Is a Better Way

When you try to make things happen by the force
of sheer will alone and nothing's happening,
you can be sure you are off track.
When something's not working, it usually means
it is not meant to work that way.
Look around . . . chances are, there is a better way.

personal pain of losing her husband to colon cancer and went so far as to have an on-air colonoscopy in 2000, which resulted in a 20 percent increase in the number of colonoscopies performed across the country, called "The Couric Effect."

Couric has received countless awards, including the prestigious Peabody, for her March 2000 "Confronting Colon Cancer" series on NBC News. She also launched the National Colorectal Cancer Research Alliance to fund medical research and conduct educational programs for prevention and early detection of the disease, the second biggest cancer killer in the U.S., and has raised around $30 million to fight colorectal and other GI (gastrointestinal) cancers by hosting extremely successful benefits.

SURRENDERING TO THE DIVINE PLAN

The fifth chakra is the bridge between the heart, traditionally thought to embody feminine values, and the head, typically believed to express masculine traits. As the center of choice, the fifth chakra is also the bridge between an individual's inner and outer worlds. This dynamic energy center is also the seat of higher energies and pure creativity.

A healthy and balanced fifth energy system is at one with the concept of divine will. Divine will is a powerful force of spiritual energy from higher dimensions that can awaken new consciousness, bring about profound realizations, and strengthen our personal will. It aligns our personal intentions with the soul to carry out our goals and purposes. Those with distorted and irregular fifth chakras tend to push against the river, trying to make deals with the universe to have things go their way. Many of us have been there in one way or another. Haven't we ever wanted it "our way or the highway?" Haven't we all ignored that still, small voice within that speaks in barely a whisper?

During my years of drinking and promiscuity, of pretense, denial, and illness, I would hear that small voice just before going to sleep or upon awakening. I would hear the voice speak from deep within me, and I would silently answer, *one day I will be free.* This was the way I put myself to sleep every night for years as a child, soothing myself without the comfort of a mother's kiss or warm embrace.

The long process of unmasking the truth took over 20 years and much work, but I now have a self I know intimately and never want to hide from again. Finding truth is a daily process of meeting that self, checking in, and talking with myself, making sure I am speaking my truth in ways that are natural and authentic. This is one way to check if you are in alignment with higher will.

Clients sometimes tell me that they think letting go of what they cannot control is an admission of failure. But for many it is exactly the opposite. Surrendering to a higher power, or simply to the concept that forces larger than ourselves are at work in the universe, is empowering. Letting go, relinquishing our need to have it our way and allowing other options and possibilities to emerge, opens us to receiving and achieving success.

Balance between voicing our desires, taking action, and allowing what is meant to happen is key here. Stop pushing . . . relax . . . allow . . . surrender.

Ask yourself the following questions:

- Do I tend to direct and orchestrate excessively?
- What is my underlying fear?
- What would happen in this particular instance if I just relaxed and let go?

Answering these questions truthfully, without pretense, can be part of our healing. *Surrender* isn't simply a word or a thought; it is a state of being. If you tend to overcontrol yourself and those around you, make your new mantra: "I choose to surrender to the powers of the universe in the running of my life, my health, my relationships, my finances, and all the small stuff, too." You will feel a lot more relaxed and you won't feel so alone.

The classic steps on the road to surrender are:

- Make no judgments.
- Have no expectations.
- Give up the need to know why.
- Trust that unscheduled events are a form of direction.

A mantra of surrender is said by members of Alcoholics Anonymous and all its offshoot organizations, called the Serenity Prayer: "God grant me the serenity to accept the things I cannot change, courage to change the things I can, and the wisdom to know the difference."

CHECKLIST

If you wonder if your throat chakra is in balance, ask yourself the following questions:

1. Do I have any of the conditions listed on page 115?
2. Am I chronically hoarse?
3. Have I had repeated sore throats or sinus problems?
4. Do I experience frequent pain in my cervical vertebrae or shoulders?
5. Do I talk too much or too loudly, stutter, or am I reluctant to speak? Am I tone deaf?
6. Am I shy?
7. Am I willing to say what I think, or am I always self-editing?
8. Do I live creatively, with a good sense of timing and rhythm?
9. Am I honest with myself and take responsibility for my own personal needs?
10. Am I able to hear and act on inner guidance?

SELF-EXPRESSION

It is important to note that speaking the truth means speaking our individual truth, which is different for each of us. Have you ever been in a meeting or lecture, listened to the words of a speaker, and afterward compared notes with others in the room? Chances are you all had a different idea of what was said. We each filter words and thoughts that come to us through our own personal perspectives and therefore hear different "truths."

A liberal person listening to a conservative talk show may think, *what a bunch of lies!* The conservative listening to a liberal politician is certainly thinking the same thing. Where is truth? This personal bias exists with everything we see, taste, smell, and feel. I love blueberries; you may hate them. If I say blueberries are delicious, is it true for you? What I experienced as hatred and rejection from my mother, she undoubtedly experienced differently. So all we can do is speak our truth— our own honest feelings about and reactions to the physical, mental, emotional, and spiritual experiences we have.

If you have problems with self-expression, you are not alone. All of us have stifled our expression to one degree or another. Many of us don't even know who we really are. If you still have work to do in learning to express your truth, journaling is a powerful tool to enhance self-discovery. It doesn't involve any great expenditure; simply find a comfortable chair, a pen, a pad of paper (or your laptop), and begin to write.

Be completely truthful in your journal. Say it like it is. If you're angry, be angry. Write it out uncensored. Be who you are. Maybe you looked polished and put together at a meeting but felt like a scared child inside. Write about that. Maybe you are going to see your wife's family, and they make you feel stupid and inferior. Write about that. Write, write, and write the truth.

The point is to be authentic. When you can trust yourself to be truthful on the pages of your journal, you can trust yourself to be truthful in the world. Just watch how your whole body relaxes as you express your truth. You've given yourself permission to be you—to speak your mind, to give voice to the truth of who you are.

If not now, when?

CHAPTER SIX

Who Is the Lie For?

Once I became sober, the flashbacks began. These were not the warm, fuzzy, "milk and cookies" memories I had always cherished. As a young girl, I checked in with Cindy on a regular basis; she kept me updated on the latest. All the delicious yet degrading and shameful things Daddy had done, he did to Cindy, not to me. When the flashbacks turned violent and perverse, I began to realize that Cindy had censored what she shared with me—and not without good reason. That censorship would now begin to dissolve bit by bit, as I was ready to face more of the truth.

For the record, Cindy was the promiscuous one, not me. The sad fact was that Cindy and I had been getting approval the best way we knew how—the way that Daddy had taught us. When I looked back at the long string of men, I realized they had all been "conquests" used to bolster my precarious self-esteem. This forced me to reorganize the way I related to men. Over time, I threw away my seductive clothes, cut off my long hair, and cleaned up my act.

Now I can relax and be myself around men. I don't need to hijack their fantasy lives or add another scalp to my belt. And blowjobs? No thanks, I gave at the office.

We've all heard the adage: "When the student is ready, the teacher will appear." I would also say that when we are ready, the pieces of our history—the stories that were lost to us or never identified—rise to the surface of consciousness. Those pieces of our stories act as our "teachers," guiding and directing us to the truth. Sometimes these pieces come as dreams, sometimes as intuitions or surprising insights, and sometimes they come in the form of illnesses, nudging gently or with life-threatening force. Whatever form they take, these lost pieces float up into awareness from the depths of our unconscious to wake us up and to help us to become more whole.

I was learning to trust in where I was being led when I went camping in the mountains east of Lake Tahoe. My husband was due to join me the next day. On my way to the campsite, I stopped at a little country store that sold herbs and natural potions. A woman of about 60 was behind the counter. She looked like a modern-day shaman, and I was searching for help with my medical problems, so I asked, "Do you do healing work?"

She looked a little startled—it wasn't something she usually broadcast—and asked how I knew.

"Oh, I just had a feeling," I said.

She invited me to her home later that day.

When I arrived, she took two long sticks that formed a "V" like a dowsing rod and pointed the odd implement at me. *Well, this is unusual,* I thought, *Never seen anyone do this kind of work before.* Having been guided to the door of many healers as

I crossed from my wild 20s into my sober 30s, I'd learned to trust the process. The woman invited me to lie down on a massage table. She then walked around me, waving her hands above my body. Afterward, she told me to stay alert and be extra gentle with myself in the coming days.

That night, I went back to my campsite, curled up, and went to sleep in my tent. In the middle of the night, I woke up with a start. I looked around, deeply startled by what I saw: there were two *me*s in the tent! The other me, whom I recognized immediately as Cindy, asked me, "Do you want to see what's in the box?"

I did not feel at all surprised by her suggestion that a box of secrets had been kept to hide something from my view. I said, "Yes, I'd love to see what's in the box."

Cindy showed me what was in the box, and I went back to sleep.

When Eric arrived in the morning, I told him about the experience. He said, "Did you look in the box?"

I said, "Yes."

"What did you see?"

"It was all about sexual abuse."

"Do you think you were sexually abused?"

"I don't know," I lied.

I had never told anyone about the abuse, not even the psychiatrist I had been seeing since I was 15. Even mentioning the experience with Cindy and the box to Eric that morning was a giant step toward lifting the gag order imposed on the truth. But I wasn't ready to reveal all the violent images and memories that were in the box just yet. I was still too embarrassed to tell anyone, even my husband. It would be a long time before I would be ready to bring those abusive experiences into the open and share them with others. Now I know that the act of sharing can often be a crucial part of healing.

The box was a sign that my intuitive mechanism was preparing to open so that I could meet the disowned parts of myself, the parts that had been in Cindy's consciousness but not mine. The box was like an intermediary hired to bring unruly members of my inner family together in one room. The "adult me" didn't understand my wild behavior, and the box was my psyche's clever way of getting my attention. It was an invitation to literally *look inside*. I love a good mystery, and over the next few years I would unravel a twisted personal whodunit as, bit-by-bit, repressed memories returned to awareness.

Intuitive ability is best understood as a skill rather than a gift bestowed on a special few. We all have innate intuitive capacities; many factors influence whether or not they develop. The shortfalls of my childhood put my nervous system on such high alert that I developed uncommon intuitive faculties. For survival reasons, I learned to read between the lines, so to speak. This capacity grew until I could read all kinds of subtle signals—the glances, gestures, and emotional nuances of people who had experiences too abhorrent to see, much less articulate. I mastered the art of feeling deeply into people, sensing their hidden motives, deepest fears, and darkest demons. I called forward the part of them they most wanted to know but had not become fully acquainted with. That part sometimes needs to be brought to consciousness for healing to take place.

My intuition served me quite well in business also. As a young attorney and hotel developer, my business partners often remarked about my uncanny ability to know all about prospective business associates and their personal predilections. Both nervous and intrigued, they would tease me, "You're so psychic," and fish around for my impressions about the outcome of a pending case or business deal, which I predicted with eerie accuracy. But this basic instinctive process was closed toward my own hidden aspects of self. When an illness developed, I often had an intuitive sense of the cause but dismissed it as absurd. I had shut down a giant part of me that was ringing an inner gong: "Wake up!"

THE SIXTH ENERGY CENTER: THE THIRD EYE CHAKRA

The sixth chakra is the source of intuition. Called the brow center—or the "third eye"—it is located between the eyebrows. When the third eye begins to open, magical synchronicities occur as we begin to see and sense connections that previously would have seemed completely coincidental. Once this center is activated, we can develop our potential for greater seeing, greater feeling, and greater hearing and move beyond the normal scope of our five senses.

The awakening of this energy center brings inspiration, insight, perception, wisdom, and vision and can lift us to unimaginable ecstasy. The question is whether or not we allow ourselves to develop this innate capacity. When our sixth energy center—the seat of higher seeing—is closed, we may feel cut off from our intuition or unable to trust what we see.

An example of how we may unconsciously block our own sight can be found in the life of Ray Charles. When he was five, Ray Charles saw his younger brother drown in an outdoor tub. Ray tried to pull his little brother out but was unable to save him. Soon after this traumatic event, he began to lose his sight. He was completely blind by the age of seven. Although Ray Charles achieved tremendous success as a musician, he suffered from heroin addiction when he was a young man. Addiction is another way of escaping what we do not want to see. While Ray Charles was able to transform his pain into music, it seems he also raised internal walls to block his view from what was painful.

The more horrendous acts my father perpetrated on me as a child severely impacted my sixth energy center: *I did not want to see my father's violence.* I had Cindy take on the job of violence management, storing the horrors away until such time as I could look at what had occurred. After many years of inner work following that first peek into "the box," I finally befriended my intuition as it related to my own life. Over time, I learned to honor my own ethical boundaries, to validate my own insights, and to make choices accordingly.

A distorted sixth chakra can manifest as poor vision, memory, or concentration, as well as closed-mindedness, nightmares, and difficulty remembering dreams. The areas of the body that relate to this energy center are the brain, neurological system, pituitary and pineal glands, eyes, and nose.

The physical diseases that can emerge as a result of distorted or closed sixth energy centers include:

- Headaches
- Upper or frontal sinus conditions
- Neurological disturbances
- Bad eyesight, glaucoma, cataracts, macular degeneration, blindness
- Stroke, hemorrhage, and brain tumor

The sixth energy center is all about discernment. Both the sixth and seventh chakras are closely linked to the endocrine glands that control the physiology of the body, from genes to the functioning of the central nervous system. The pituitary gland, often referred to as the "master" gland because it influences every other endocrine gland, is also associated with the sixth energy center. This gland provides a connection between the brain and the immune system and influences the way trauma is experienced and recorded in the brain, which can lead to allergies or illness later on.

Intuition or "second sight" is often disdained in a culture that views the rational mind as king. Our Western cultural tradition relies on the intellect and rejects intuitive gifts as hocus-pocus. The general public, however, has become intrigued with the unseen in recent years, and popular television shows like *Medium* and *Psychic Detectives* reflect a growing appetite for these capabilities. As a culture, we are becoming more comfortable with the idea that intuition is a real phenomenon that we can develop to our benefit. Each of us has access to a psychic detective in the form of our intuition if we choose to open and develop this innate ability.

As my own healing pilgrimage moved me to higher levels of awareness, I was able to look back at the moment Cindy showed me the box and see that it was my psyche calling for integration. The time had come to put together the parts of my split consciousness that Cindy had kept in the box. I was ready to see a more complete picture of my father and mother—the good, the bad, and the ugly.

UNITY CONSCIOUSNESS

From the perspective of unity consciousness, we are all one, and everything we can say about someone else can also be said of us. Even the tyrants of the world reflect a tyrannical aspect of each of us. The more we are able to see beyond the me-versus-you, us-versus-them duality to the deeper truth of unity, the more we can heal the illusion that we are separate from others.

At one of my public healing events, a woman raised her hand for individual attention. Laura, who had just turned 30, came to the front of the room and revealed that she had cystic fibrosis. This respiratory disease had already cost her both of her lungs. Following a double lung transplant, her body had begun to reject the new lungs. She was being pumped full of steroids to counteract the rejection and did not look well. She reported that she had suffered a stroke several months after her lung transplant.

I dropped deeply into Laura's body/mind and discerned that she was holding an unconscious thought that the transplanted lungs were "not her." This thought was inadvertently creating the very rejection that was killing her. Gently pointing out that we are not separate, but all one, I suggested that she welcome the new lungs as a real part of her own body. A light came on in her awareness as she embraced the idea. Laura immediately began to relax. She confessed she had been in a fear pattern since the transplant nearly a year earlier. The powerful truth for her came with recognizing that only she could make the shift from fear to gratitude. At the same time, I was able to accelerate her healing by calming the immune response that was rejecting the lungs.

SEE NO EVIL

Mike came to see me after being diagnosed with glaucoma and receiving a recommendation for laser eye surgery. He was worried about losing his eyesight and thus was motivated to seek help. He had barely shut my office door before his story came pouring out.

For nearly 16 years, Mike had been the manager and co-owner of a small boutique hotel in a resort area. His out-of-town business partner had financed the purchase of the hotel and owned half of the operation. Three years earlier, Mike had married a beautiful, loving, gentle woman named Emily. His new wife was good to him, and Mike was thrilled when Emily expressed interest in working at the hotel. She had an easy way with the public and turned out to have a good head for business. Within a few months, Mike promoted her to front desk manager. Not long after Emily began working at the front desk, however, Mike noticed that the books didn't always balance at the end of the day. The amounts missing from the till were small at first; later they were larger.

An experienced manager, Mike intuitively knew that the discrepancies could only be traced to Emily. Intimidated by his

See No Evil?

The image of the three monkeys—
see no evil, speak no evil, hear no evil—
has been seared into our cultural consciousness.
At some level, we still believe it a virtue to not see or speak
or hear the truth. In fact, our emotional, physical,
and mental health lies in the balance.
See, speak, and hear the truth—deal with "what is."

own intuition, he convinced himself that he couldn't be sure which employee might be embezzling. However, Mike could not so readily convince himself that he wasn't cheating his partner by refusing to address the problem, and this conflict festered inside him. Mike was not surprised when I connected this conflict to his eyes. I explained that the huge effort he had to put into *not seeing* was placing an extraordinary amount of pressure on his optic nerve.

When Mike and Emily first started dating, she had told him quite proudly that she was a "creative bookkeeper." As a college student, she made ends meet by holding garage sales for her neighbors and keeping more than her share of the money. Later, she graduated to filching small sums from a retail store she had managed. She justified her behavior, saying it fairly compensated her for the unpaid overtime her managerial duties required. Mike considered this stealing and thought Emily was being dishonest with herself, but he never said as much to her.

When people get married they buy the part they can see in each other, but they also buy the part they can't or don't want to see. Mike sensed trouble in how Emily conducted herself with the money that she held in trust for others, but he chose not to address it. She downplayed her petty thievery, insisting "everybody does it." When she challenged Mike, he had to admit he had done things like that as well. Emily seemed to have no guilt or shame and thought her actions were perfectly okay. In her opinion, minor white-collar crime was a way of beating an unfair system.

From his point of view, the only system she was "beating" was her own. He believed she was hurting them both but failed to tell her this.

After clearing, balancing, and charging Mike's energy field, I told him that his sight problems would continue to get worse if he did not tell his wife the truth about how he saw her behavior. Confessing that he was afraid she would leave him, he realized after some reflection that losing his eyesight and his own integrity was too high a price to pay. He was also concerned that his business partner might find out and take legal action. He finally decided that his marriage could not survive if he did not address these concerns.

Mike went home and told Emily he wasn't comfortable with her role in his business and wanted her to find another job. He told her that he knew she'd been stealing and could not allow her to take from the business any longer. A huge fight broke out between them. Mike held his ground, however, and Emily went back to her previous position in retail sales. Once the dust settled, Emily admitted to being impressed with the line Mike had drawn in the sand. His insistence on integrity brought an unexpected gift to their relationship, and Emily began to re-evaluate her own behavior. She later admitted to Mike that she realized her actions stemmed from old anger at her mother—the first authority figure in her life who had treated her unfairly. Getting one over on authority figures and taking what didn't belong to her was her way of feeling powerful. Mike's action not only helped his own healing, but also awakened a new awareness in Emily, an unexpected bonus.

Some months later, Mike's ophthalmologist advised him that the pressure in his eyes had decreased and surgery was no longer needed. Mike is certain the turnaround was directly linked to his willingness to both see and take a stand regarding his wife's embezzlement.

Lies that remain hidden from awareness or concealed from a spouse create tension and strain on the relationship. Embracing the truth and accepting the inevitable results involve both risk and reward. In Mike's case, the resulting release of tension allowed his condition to resolve. *Truth heals.*

CREATIVE VISION

Suppressing the truth can also affect creativity, an aspect of the sixth chakra. A successful screenwriter, James had made a fortune in action and adventure movies. He came to me struggling with writer's block. Previously, James had demonstrated a remarkable ability to take an idea from concept to creation in record time. But a year earlier, that very ability had suddenly dried up. He'd lost all inspiration and could no longer complete a project. Not only was his industry reputation at stake, he also felt very concerned about his finances. His family had grown accustomed to the standard of living his professional success provided. His wife thought James just needed to relax and suggested they take more regular breaks and day trips, even longer vacations. Yet nothing seemed to recharge his creative juices.

When James first came to my office, he was reluctant and skeptical about healing work. He confessed that he'd come in with a "nothing to lose" attitude, but he had serious doubts that I would be able to help. I saw that James's sixth energy center was completely closed. When I queried him as to when the problem with his creative process began, he told me his story. A few years earlier, a producer approached him about an action/adventure movie James had pitched early in his career. Although James had outgrown the story, the producer offered a sizable salary, believing the project could be a blockbuster. James had grown up poor and always prided himself on having acquired wealth at a young age. He rarely turned down a project if significant payment was involved, and, despite a clear message from his intuition not to take this one, he accepted.

James completed the script, but spent a harrowing two years embroiled in a hornet's nest. He felt he had signed his life—and his idea—away. He was also angry with himself for having been lured by money and the promise of a hit. Although successful as a writer, he didn't feel he was an "A-lister" and envied those in the industry who were. I saw in his energy field that James was not aligned with the subject matter of the film. The story was exploitive and full of gratuitous violence. James had long since abandoned the anger of his youth, which had given birth to the story many years before. I asked him whether he felt he had crossed his own ethical boundaries by working on this project. He reflected a moment and looked at me, confused. I asked him more directly if he felt good about this story.

At first he hemmed and hawed, then he confessed that he did not care for the storyline anymore. He no longer believed violence was an acceptable way to solve problems and felt the film projected an irresponsible message. When James made the connection between his disapproval for his own project and the feeling that he had compromised his beliefs for money and fame, something inside him seemed to relax. He was able to forgive himself for making a choice that was less than honorable in his own mind. He realized that he could no longer work on projects that were not aligned with his heart; he now wanted to use his talent to deliver positive messages. His children were his inspiration and he no longer wanted to write or produce "schlock."

After several sessions, James felt drawn to sit down at his computer and write. His muse returned—stronger than ever.

Listen to Who You Are

When we listen to our intuition, heed our own morality,
and take action in alignment with our ethics,
we can walk with our heads held high.
When we don't, we suffer.
Eventually, lies that we tell ourselves eat away at us
and diminish our health. Be true to you.

Today he only commits to creative projects when his inner guidance gives him the green light.

I have often seen this scenario in artists—musicians, painters, photographers, writers, and dancers: if they become divorced from their essence, from their true purpose, they lose inspiration and become less effective creatively. Feeling true to ourselves and listening to that still, small voice inside is vital to living a meaningful and joyous life.

A BALANCED SIXTH CHAKRA

When our sixth energy centers are in balance, we keep an open mind and seek the truth. We sense the interconnectedness of humankind and are willing to look for guidance within ourselves and at our psychic experiences. Seeing clairvoyantly is only one aspect of this center, and its importance is often overemphasized and overrated. Clairvoyance, or the ability to see beyond this plane, is actually the least reliable of the subtle senses. Instead, an ideal sixth chakra has the power of discernment—inner and outer discretion—at its disposal.

Albert Einstein, the great scientist, was also a great seer. His sixth energy center was wide open. He is remembered for his genius and for recognizing the importance of intuitive guidance in the invention and creation of new technologies, sciences, paradigms, beliefs, and philosophies. Einstein said, "The most important decision you will ever make is whether the universe is friendly or not." He believed that the single most vital quality for human beings to develop is imagination;

as he said, "Imagination is greater than knowledge." Without imagination and intuition as its guiding force, our world would become stagnant and inert. We could say the same of our lives: without the magic and inspiration of our imagination, our lives would not have the sheen or radiance they do when our sixth energy centers are fully open and accessed.

Another visionary is Al Gore. The former vice president dropped out of the spotlight for a while after his election upset in the 2000 presidential race; he became a visiting professor at several universities and an environmental advisor for corporations before being in the spotlight again with his Oscar-winning documentary, *An Inconvenient Truth*. The film features Gore's lectures and scientific research about environmental change, exposing the audience to his well-informed and disturbing vision of what the future has in store for us concerning global warming. He was awarded the 2007 Nobel Peace Prize for "efforts to build up and disseminate greater knowledge about man-made climate change, and to lay the foundations for the measures that are needed to counteract such change."

Steven Spielberg, the three-time Academy Award winner, producer, and highest grossing filmmaker of all time, is another true visionary with a wide open sixth chakra. Despite being refused admission three times to the USC film school because of his C grade average, Spielberg never lost sight of his goal to direct films. Looking in many different directions—from blockbuster horror, sci-fi, and adventure films to dramas dealing with difficult historical issues like the Holocaust, slavery, and terrorism—his films have made over $8 billion around the world. Many of his films deal with ordinary people who come into contact with extraordinary beings or circumstances, and like his family-friendly films, Spielberg seems to see the world with a sense of childlike wonder. He brings that sense of faith and optimism to sick children through the Starlight Starbright Children's Foundation, dedicated to improving quality of life for children with chronic or life-threatening medical conditions through hi-tech entertainment and education programs.

CHECKLIST

If you wonder whether your sixth chakra is open and balanced, you might ask yourself if you are feeling at peace with all areas of your life. The following questions will help you determine this:

1. Am I listening to and following my inner guidance?
2. Do I have any of the conditions listed on pages 138?
3. Do I dream, and can I remember my dreams?
4. Do I have an illness whose onset coincided with an emotional event or loss that I did not want to fully embrace?
5. Do I anticipate positive outcomes or negative ones?
6. Do I have a habit of denying or ignoring what's true?
7. Am I honoring my own ethics and moral obligations?
8. Can I see more than one way to address an issue?

Visualizing goals, dreams, and outcomes is a wonderful self-healing technique for the sixth energy center. Regularly spend time resting with your eyes closed, picturing the exact outcome you desire, whether at work, at home, or even in your golf game. Opening yourself to this energy center opens to the wisdom of your higher self and to your more refined inner guidance system. Affirm your willingness to listen to your own inner direction.

Expressing the truth about who we are and what we really want is the key to peace and healthy living. Listening to ourselves and acknowledging what we really feel allows us to change what is not working and to live in a more meaningful, purposeful way. If we are not willing to listen to or see our truth, the question that we really need to ask is, *who is the lie for?*

I often guide workshop participants to ask their own higher wisdom for guidance and signs that they are on the right path. I encourage them to listen for internal messages regarding purpose and direction and to visualize positive or peaceful outcomes. This may require putting self-interest aside and instead embracing the greater good for all.

CHAPTER SEVEN

It's All About Trust

Rare is the five-year-old who understands the meaning of the word vocation, and yet I was quite certain of mine—to be a nun. Parading around in a makeshift habit fashioned out of sheets and a giant rosary tied around my waist, I'd slip a pebble in my shoe and put a piece of burlap against my skin for penance. Envious of the altar boys who were learning Latin, I hid in the choir loft during their lessons and mastered the language of the Mass in secret.

One rainy day when I was eight, I went to my favorite hiding spot in the choir loft during lunch recess. I pictured the Virgin Mary before me and closed my eyes in prayer. When I heard Father Fitzgerald's footsteps on the stairs, I knew this meant trouble.

"What are you doing up here, my child?" he asked. I darted for the stairs, but he caught me by a braid. He held me in place, one alabaster hand on each arm. He smelled like fried potatoes. His long black cassock was buttoned all the way to the floor;

his black shoes were as shiny as his greasy hair. "You little temptress," he whispered. "I know how you've been tempting your father, bless his soul. It is my duty to straighten you out." He raised his cassock and pushed me down on my knees.

The Virgin Mary appeared before me. The folds of her gown rippled like waves as she came close. A bright blue light sparkled all around her. After some time, she disappeared. I was once again alone.

My lifelong fascination with the miraculous was fueled and fed by Catholicism. Perhaps in an attempt to escape the pain at home, I immersed myself in the stories of Jesus, Mary, and all the saints and prayed fervently that their statues would come to life. Sometimes they did.

Communing with spirit became my salvation, and I prayed on my knees at every turn. When the parish priest, to whom my father had presumably confessed his sins, forced me to my knees, I was too young to understand. I assumed I was being punished for being bad and became even more abject.

By the time I was 15, however, I had become angry and rebelled against the church, rejecting all things spiritual. The voice of spirit was far from my consciousness. It attempted to speak at various times through my intuition, but I rarely listened.

Looking back, I see a grand master plan at work. But during my 20s, I never imagined that my destiny was to become a healer and a master of energy. If someone had told me that, I would have laughed. Me? Are you kidding?

It all began one summer after Eric and I had married, when I suffered a horrible ache in my low back. I tried treating the problem with acupuncture, massage, and chiropractic, all to no avail. When my acupuncturist suggested I see a healer who lived in the mountains above Santa Barbara, I gave Eric the "let's go" look; he scooped me up from the acupuncture table, laid me flat in the back of our van, and drove off in search of this healer.

When we arrived at the door of a little cottage in the middle of nowhere, a handsome young man who looked more like a surfer than a healer greeted us. I was stunned by the light in Peter's eyes. He looked at me and asked, "Yes?"

I was about to say, "I'm here because of my aching back," but something else came out of my mouth. "I am here for God consciousness."

Without skipping a beat, he replied, "Well, you've come to the right place. You're already in the birth process. I'll be your midwife."

I lay on a table as Peter moved his hands above my body. I saw colors and shapes and wave patterns and felt like I was spiraling up and up and up. He asked me to mimic his breathing. My breathing accelerated as I felt myself leave my body. In my mind's eye, I saw a man approach. I thought, *who is that?*

As he came closer, I saw a halo above his head. *I know that man,* I said to myself as the figure walked right up to me. When I recognized who it was, I heard my breath draw in with a slight gasp. It was Jesus. For years, I had longed for this—to see Him and speak with Him. Now here He was, right in front of me.

I wept as something at the core of my being cracked open and spilled out. Just as people in the movies see their lives reel before them when on the verge of death, all the sins of my life flashed before me—everything I had taken part in, all the ways I had dishonored myself.

Full of self-recrimination and horror, I cried out, "I am so sorry, I am so terribly sorry. I did such a lousy job of my life until now. Please forgive me."

My life was never to be the same. When I left the little cottage, everything was different: the sky was brighter, trees were greener, and their branches seemed to bend down to greet me. Everything shimmered and sparkled and smiled.

As we drove home toward our ranch, I asked Eric to take me to the stables. I had not seen my horse for a long time and wanted to say hello. When we pulled up, I started talking with the lady who ran the barn. She asked if I'd heard the latest and suddenly we were in the thick of it, passing judgment like two women with nothing better to do than gossip. Within moments, I realized, *Oh my God, I went*

Trust Life, Trust God

In this moment, do you trust life?
Do you trust that you are loved, protected, and supported?
Do you trust that everything is working out
for your highest good? If you don't, ask for more trust.
Speak it: "Show me how to trust more!"
Then watch for signs that your life (and God) is listening.

back to my old habits so quickly. This is going to be harder than I thought!

We can be set on the launch pad of the divine, but it's up to us to project the divine into the world. Although we still have the same bodies and the same old habits, it's our job to become impeccable in how we live. As I discovered only minutes after my miraculous opening to spirit, being human *and* impeccable wasn't going to be easy.

I went home that day and did nothing. I stopped working. The next day and the next and the next I did nothing. For the next six months I did nothing but float through my days absorbed in universal consciousness. I sat in a big old tree, stared at the sky, and communed with nature. I meditated and prayed eight to ten hours a day. I felt a connection to the moon and sometimes made my bed under the stars. I had visions and conversations with Jesus, the Virgin Mary, and other representatives of the divine feminine. I felt I'd been enrolled in a university of the spirit and was being taught 24 hours a day. It was the most beautiful experience of my life. Eric would return from work at the end of the day, walk to where I sat in the garden, and say, "You're sitting in exactly the same place I left you this morning." I was totally connected to Source, with the God consciousness I had long sought: that sense of oneness with all that was and is and ever will be.

A long period of testing began once I reluctantly moved back into the world of the mundane. Returning to work as an attorney and hotel developer, my connection to the realm of spirit became elusive. Weaving between the two worlds was a treacherous process in the best of times. I often forgot what I had learned during all those months spent in stillness and absorption. Many times I failed to meet the ideals I had set for myself and lost sight of the luminous insights I had gained. Further tests and challenges came, compelling me to forge an ever-deepening connection with the divine through pain wrought by my own error.

THE SEVENTH ENERGY CENTER: THE CROWN CHAKRA

The seventh energy center at the top of the head is called the "crown chakra." This is our connection with spirit, our higher power, and the universe. It connects deeply within the brain to the pineal and pituitary glands and relates to the hypothalamus and the central nervous system. The crown chakra also links to the immune system as it relates to the psyche and emotions. The unification of human and divine occurs here in what is sometimes referred to as the *superconscious*—the place of the visionary mind, beyond time and space. This energy center opens outward and upward, pulling light energy in from above and flooding us with an experience of transcendence. We are no longer merely human when this center of energy is awakened; an enormous power lights up our consciousness.

Distortion of the seventh energy center may result in learning difficulties, rigid belief systems, spiritual addiction, cynicism, apathy, confusion, over-intellectualization, or over-identification with one's own ego.

Religious cults both stem from and seed imbalances in the seventh chakra. By force-feeding their belief systems to members, they perpetuate lies and misinformation. The standard in-group, out-group, us-versus-them mentality is used by cults to abuse and control its members psychologically, emotionally, spiritually, and even sexually—all in the name of "religion." Such cults are famous for exploiting women, the young and impressionable, and children. Often, leaders of extreme religious cults are people who have themselves been traumatized or misguided by controlling and tyrannical patriarchs. Among some Mormon fundamentalists, 14-year-old girls are forced to marry 50-year-old men who already have numerous wives. This is a good example of a sect that practices exploitation under the guise of "religious belief."

Psychedelic drugs also seed imbalances in the seventh chakra. Some have thought that drugs like LSD, "magic" mushrooms, and ayahuasca could help achieve transcendence—a state of peace, love, oneness, and mastery. However, as a great sage in India said, "LSD lets you peek in through the window at Christ, but it won't let you meet Him face-to-face." Ultimately, drugs can make a person feel cut off and disconnected. Drugs force the chakras to open and expand, allowing users to experience perceptions beyond their normal range. Unfortunately, when the drug wears off, the chakras close down and contract more tightly than before. Prayer, meditation, music, and nature are far more powerful tools for achieving a real connection to the divine.

The diseases and disorders that may manifest as a result of an unbalanced or distorted seventh energy center include:

- Anxiety and depression
- Bipolar disorder
- Coma or amnesia
- Headache, migraine
- Stroke
- Brain tumor
- Epilepsy
- Multiple sclerosis
- Parkinson's disease
- Attention Deficit Disorder (ADD) and dyslexia
- Cognitive delusions
- ALS (Lou Gehrig's disease)
- Mental illness, schizophrenia, and multiple personality disorder
- Dementia or Alzheimer's disease

Carrie Fisher, the daughter of Debbie Reynolds and Eddie Fisher (who left when Carrie was two to marry Elizabeth Taylor), is a good example of someone who has struggled with a distorted seventh chakra. Diagnosed with bipolar disorder while in her early teens, the condition was probably an inheritance from her bipolar mother. Another inheritance was addiction, as her father was addicted to drugs, gambling, and women. Habits of how to handle problems are passed down just as genes are. Cocaine and alcohol abuse eventually led to an overdose and rehab, which resulted in Carrie's first best-selling novel, *Postcards From the Edge*.

Fisher once again went into treatment when she recognized early signs that a combination of prescribed medication for her bipolar condition and pain medication from dental implants was leading her back into addiction. The iconic role of Princess Leia in the original *Star Wars* trilogy long behind her, Fisher more recently took her troubled past—which included a marriage to Paul Simon and a child by a man who forgot to tell her he was gay—and her considerable skills as a writer and turned them into a one-woman show called *Wishful Drinking*.

In the days when I was seeing a psychiatrist for the bipolar tendencies I had at that time, I told him that I had discovered a great key for dealing with being bipolar—alcohol! The psychiatrist said, "Well, I should tell you that that probably won't work out too well."

Therapy worked out well for actress Lorraine Bracco, who ironically wound up playing the psychiatrist who treats Tony Soprano for depression on the HBO hit show, *The Sopranos*. Her own depression came from a pileup of difficulties in her life, including a divorce, another failed relationship, a battle over custody, a sick child, and a lot of debt. Eventually helped by therapy and medication, Bracco wants to lift the stigma associated with depression and bring it to public attention.

THE MYSTERIOUS WORKINGS
OF THE BRAIN

Those who suffer illnesses related to the seventh chakra, from dementia to brain tumors and stroke, often have a distortion in that energy center. At one of my public events, a man was desperate to have his wife healed from Alzheimer's disease. She was a lovely woman of about 65 with a look of beatific peace on her face. Alzheimer's had slowly rendered her completely absent from the present moment. Her husband was angry and scared, and I had compassion for him. On the one hand, he demanded that I help her, while on the other hand, he repeatedly asserted that nothing would help. The other participants were uncomfortable with this man's presence, yet he seemed unaware of his effect on those around him. I saw that his wife was at the level of a two-year-old. She felt treasured and loved by the work I was doing. She felt the light of healing pass through her but did not want to come back to this reality. She was happy where she was.

With people who develop Alzheimer's, I often see an inability to bear the present. They begin to slip out of their minds, a little more each day. Clairvoyantly, their brains look like Swiss cheese. Alzheimer's sufferers find holes for slipping out of the present, which they find untenable for whatever reason, until they finally slip out permanently and cannot find their way back.

When people absent themselves through Alzheimer's, they go to places where they can explore the parts of themselves they have previously denied. A relative of mine had been very prudish and hypercritical of sexual expression during her lifetime. When she developed Alzheimer's, she became ultra-flirtatious with men, pulling up her skirt in seductive ways, and acting out her sexuality with none of her usual self-containment and control.

The brain is indeed a mystery. When the energy in the seventh chakra ceases to flow as it should, the brain's "revenge" can be harsh. Jack was a successful salesman and type A personality. By the time he came to me, Jack had already had surgery for a virulent brain tumor. His surgeon found that much of the tumor was inoperable, and essentially told Jack he'd best go home and write his will. Rejecting the doctor's prognosis, Jack chose to work with me and focus on healing rather than dying. Incredibly receptive to my suggestions, he took up yoga and altered his diet. We identified the underlying causes of his brain tumor as the stress produced by the crazy pace he kept and a hostile relationship with his mother, a constant source of stress he had been ignoring for a very long time.

Jack reduced his workload, embarked upon a calmer and more serene lifestyle and his health began to improve, The one piece that remained unresolved, however, was his relationship with his mother. Emotionally and physically abusive toward him as a child and disapproving at every turn once he'd grown into adulthood, his mother was the one person he simply could not forgive. He spent little time around her, even foregoing extended family gatherings and celebrations to avoid her. Through our efforts, Jack began the work of forgiving his mother, an excruciating process given the severity of the abuse he had experienced throughout his life. As Jack took the first painful steps toward healing, I explained to him that forgiveness and reconciliation were not the same thing and that he need never see his mother again—should he so choose. As his healing progressed, the tumor in his brain diminished.

That, however, is not the happy conclusion to his story. Unexpectedly, Jack accepted an invitation to visit his brother and mother. He found his mother's old hostility toward him as painful as ever. He was angered and, upon his return, told me that he could not forgive her—not ever. Within three months he was dead. Perhaps Jack allowed his rage to consume him and sought to punish his mother with his death.

Another way an unbalanced seventh energy center can manifest in the body is in the form of a stroke. Maggie was 48 years old when she came to see me; she had already suffered two strokes. The first occurred right after finalizing a brutal divorce; the second followed in short order. We have all heard of the *evil eye:* malevolent intent directed toward us that can impact our health. In Maggie's case, her ex-husband hated her and sent a negative vector of force to her brain with every breath he took. He used to call her "brain-dead" and that was exactly the energy he sent her, both consciously and unconsciously, through his thoughts and words.

When I explained to Maggie that her ex-husband was sending a strong, negative energy to her, she knew exactly what I meant. She had always felt the intensity of his control when she was married, even when she was away from him—and could still feel it. She did not believe that his hateful energy could actually injure her though. I confirmed that it could if she allowed her fear to control her. We cleared her brain of the remnants of his negativity, and I taught her a powerful technique to protect her from his energy in the future.

Even though distance has no effect on thought patterns, I asked Maggie if she was willing to cease all contact with her ex. I sensed that, in her case, disconnecting completely was important for her healing. She had no problem doing so and was quite relieved to feel supported in releasing this toxic relationship from her life. I was pleased when Maggie announced she was moving to the East Coast to live with an old college friend.

Energy-based medicine reveals that we are as vulnerable to invisible hazards as we are to bodily threats; it looks beyond the physical to contributing factors in the psychological and spiritual dimensions. Little is yet understood in mainstream medicine about the power of thought to affect the body; integrative medicine—the merger of traditional and alternative modalities—is beginning to broaden conventional medicine's perspective.

FALLING INTO GRACE

Destiny comes to us as small taps at our consciousness. If those little signals don't get through to us, destiny may hit us over the head with greater force. Sometimes destiny smashes through the wall we have built between ordinary life and our divine purpose by bringing us to the brink of death or madness. Life as we have known it can cease entirely in such a passage, and yet the arms of grace extend and catch us where we fall.

I am convinced that we can run from our destiny for only so long before God makes it impossible for us to continue doing so. My illusions were shattered and I subsequently fell into the arms of grace when my husband fell while mountain climbing. The constant fear that I would lose Eric as a result of this accident pitched me into terror but eventually revealed the path I travel today.

We had just returned from a climbing expedition in the Himalayas and were set to do an afternoon climb at Lover's Leap, not far from our home in the Sierra Nevada Mountains. Climbing gave me an extraordinary sense of freedom and steadied my frantic mind, so much that I told Eric on our first date, "Climbing is my new psychotherapy." We had made this climb many times before, but something told me not to go that morning. I ignored my trepidation, believing as I did that Eric was invincible and I immortal. We were famous in climbing circles for our reckless habits of starting late up the mountain and never climbing with another team. We tempted fate all the time and always walked away exhilarated. *Why worry?* I dismissed my premonition of harm.

That particular morning, Eric and I had a petty argument on the drive up the mountain. By the time we arrived at base camp, we were barely speaking. When Eric suggested I lead the climb, a flash of fear went through me. Was he not feeling up to par? I decided not to ask and started up the first pitch. After a few feet, the cracks branched; I took the easier right crack. The wind was cold and unrelenting. The first 150 feet took me an hour to ascend. Rather than the usual adrenaline rush I'd always experienced upon making the first ledge, I felt exhausted. A nagging voice in my head whispered fearful thoughts, but I kept pushing them away.

Eric shouted up at me with directions on how to set the belay, the safety backup system. But the wind carried his voice down the canyon. Cold and impatient, I set the nut in a hurry. I should have set an extra nut or two, but I set the single nut and waved him on, as he always said the belay was "pure theory" anyway.

Both of us knew that a good fall could pull out the safety equipment and cause both climbers to "ground out," a euphemism for smashing into the ground. We had attended the funeral of a fellow climber earlier that year.

My hands on the rope that connected us were completely numb. Why hadn't I thought to bring belay gloves? Eric started climbing and took the harder left crack with a difficult overhang. After a long period of waiting, I heard his voice below me. He was close now, just below the overhang. His next move required tremendous agility and a well-positioned belay. My intuition finally got my attention and for a moment my heart stopped. I called out to Eric, "Stop! I need to reset the belay!"

He refused, saying, "There's no way to stop, I'm coming on!" A moment later, I heard him cry out, "Falling!" The rope began running in the wrong direction, tearing through the skin and muscles of my ungloved hands. I watched helplessly as his body hurtled through the air toward the ground below. He hit the ground with a loud thud. The sound of his moan carried up to me. Then there was only silence.

I began to scream for help. It would take me hours to rig an emergency belay and descend. Eric needed help *now*. It was a Sunday in April; I knew other climbers were on the mountain. After what seemed an endless stretch of time, voices from somewhere in the canyon answered my screams. Four men appeared below me. Eric was alive, they said, but unconscious. Two of the climbers hiked out to get help while the other two tended to Eric. I began a dangerous solo rappel to the ground.

At the hospital, the doctors stabilized Eric and he regained consciousness. After a few days had passed, the attending neurosurgeon explained that a closed head injury of the type Eric had sustained was not treatable. All we could do was wait and allow his brain to heal. At the end of the first year, Eric's condition had worsened. He could walk but could not read or sleep. He couldn't be in a room with lights or TV on or tolerate riding in a car. He moved between fits of choking, when I was sure he would die in my arms, to fits of rage—both a result of the closed head injury. His descent into depression, another side effect, was agonizing for both of us.

Our home, which had been a way station between climbing and skiing trips around the world, became our prison. I brought my law office home and pretended I no longer wanted to climb or ski. Eric needed me now; my place was at his side. He had rescued me time and again from drunken sprees, manic episodes, and my own periods of deep depression. He had forgiven me repeatedly and had loved me through the worst—now it was my turn. My thrill-seeking life narrowed down to nothing but work and caring for Eric. Day in and day out: work and care for Eric, work and care for Eric. I needed to do it, I wanted to do it, but my inner resources were in short supply. On a daily basis, I felt certain I'd go mad if something didn't give.

Open Your Mind

"The mind is like a parachute.
It works better when it's open."—
an old adage and a useful reminder of the truth.
Keep your mind open, fresh, available to the new.
Rigid, immovable thinking hardens us and
disconnects us from the divine.
The divine is fluid and invites us to flow with it.

Within a few weeks of the accident, I had begun to develop a speech impediment—a reaction, no doubt, to stress. When I spoke about this to my sister-in-law, a speech therapist, she cautioned that I could have a brain tumor. I stopped talking altogether after that! Overnight, I developed food allergies. Within a year, I began having ominous symptoms in my reproductive organs and finally reached out for help. I sat in the gynecologist's office, rocking back and forth and crying hysterically, "I can't handle my husband's head injury. I can't handle it for another moment."

My body and spirit were nearing complete breakdown, but I kept trying to find some help, any help, for Eric. Each day I pushed further. Alternative healing modalities offered hope—and ultimately the answer to our prayers. But it took Eric's accident for destiny to get my attention. I did not value myself enough to listen, but I listened on behalf of someone I deeply loved. God *had* me then—my ears, eyes, and heart were wide open. The quest that would eventually bring me to my life's work had begun. Over the next 20 years, numerous teachers and healers guided me to a clear and open connection with the divine.

The long, arduous period of time it took for Eric to recover was my own long, dark night of the soul. It took going to the depths of human despair and hopelessness for me to learn how to surrender. The hard-driving person I had been was forced to soften and let go at a deeper level than I had ever known or imagined possible. I had to connect with and release my own rage. I had to face what my mother and father had done and had to face all of who they were. I had to forgive, forgive, forgive and, most importantly, find forgiveness for myself.

AN OPEN CROWN CHAKRA

The actualization of a fully balanced and integrated seventh energy center occurs through *surrender*—a crucial concept in an awakened energy system. The great paradox of paradoxes occurs with this surrender to the divine. By giving up and giving ourselves over to something greater, we relinquish our small egos to a more expansive purpose. All good things flow to us as a result. Here in the seventh chakra we learn the truth: There is truly nothing to seek. Everything is within us. We are all connected. We are all one. To know *that*, intimately and deeply, is to know *all*.

A person with an open crown energy center is a beautiful sight to behold. I met a man at one of my seminars who was an inspiring example of someone with an open seventh energy center. He sat in the second row near the front of the room, waving his arm wildly, hoping to be chosen from the crowd. He was about 30 years old, over six feet tall, and quite attractive. When I pointed to him, he jumped to his feet and walked toward me with a lopsided gait. I asked, "How can I help you?"

He said he had been in an accident in Montana when his truck went over a cliff. He was thrown from the truck before it rolled onto his leg. Several days passed before someone found him at the bottom of the ravine. The leg had to be amputated, and the foot on his remaining leg suffered nerve damage.

I sat down on a small step next to him and took his foot in my lap. When I asked what the medical profession had told him about the damage to his remaining foot, he said, "I have no insurance. I have not consulted anyone."

I said, "I'm quite impressed with how you have handled this challenge."

He smiled and replied, "I'm really trying." And it was clear that he was. He was in acceptance rather than self-pity, resentment, or resignation. His level of awareness and his openness at the sixth and seventh chakras were quite profound. Everyone in the room was moved by this man's presence.

I worked to refine his connection to Source. Because he already had a very open connection spiritually, I helped accentuate and deepen that link by taking away any worry or anxiety that remained in his field. Fear, anxiety, and anger shut down our connection to the divine. This is one reason we pray or use techniques that allow us to release emotions that otherwise block the light coming down through the crown chakra. Balancing our crown chakra helps us to live openly, fully on our paths, and selflessly contribute to the greater good.

Someone with an integrated seventh chakra is Bono, U2's lead singer/songwriter, who has put his fame and wealth to work in the service of AIDS awareness, poverty relief in Africa, third world debt forgiveness, and action in troubled areas such as Darfur. This Rock and Roll Hall of Famer has a trophy case heavy with Grammys and a Golden Globe, but he has also received numerous honors for his ongoing humanitarian efforts, including three Nobel Peace Prize nominations, the Légion d'Honneur in France, and an honorary Knight Commander of the Order of the British Empire.

Bono, who has spoken about his admiration for Dr. Martin Luther King, Jr., has been called "the face of fusion philanthropy" based on his success in enlisting help from across a diverse spectrum of government officials, religious institutions, philanthropic organizations, media, and the business world. He spearheaded the Project Red campaign, persuading major commercial enterprises such as Gap, Armani, Converse, and American Express to donate one percent of Red product customer sales to the Global Fund to fight AIDS, tuberculosis, and malaria. During a trip to Africa in which he championed debt relief, Bono told reporters, "A fundamental human right is the ability to start again, to break free from the sins of the father." He has also spoken of turning "dreaming into doing."

One actor who has channeled his own crown chakra distortions into helping others is Henry Winkler, the "Fonz" of *Happy Days* fame. Winkler grew up with what he called "a high level of low self-esteem" as he struggled with academics because of his dyslexia. To help others with this problem, he co-authored a series of 12 children's books about a fourth grader, called *Hank Zipzer, the World's Greatest Underachiever*, which has helped millions of children with learning disabilities. He is also involved with the Annual Cerebral Palsy Telethon, the Epilepsy Foundation of America, the annual

Toys for Tots campaign, the National Committee for Arts for the Handicapped, and the Special Olympics.

Another person whose actions indicate tremendous insight is celebrated actor Michael J. Fox, who hasn't let Parkinson's disease destroy his spirit. In his autobiography, *Lucky Man,* the scrappy "army brat" wrote this about the disease: " . . . this unexpected crisis forced a fundamental life decision: adopt a siege mentality—or embark upon a journey. Whatever it was—courage? acceptance? wisdom?—that finally allowed me to go down the second road (after spending a few disastrous years on the first) was unquestionably a gift—and absent this neurophysiological catastrophe, I would never have opened it, or been so profoundly enriched. That's why I consider myself a lucky man." The Michael J. Fox Foundation for Parkinson's Research has funded over $115 million in research for the development of a cure for Parkinson's disease.

CHECKLIST

If you wonder whether your crown center is open and balanced, start by consulting the following checklist.

1. Do I have any of the conditions listed on pages 159?
2. Am I inclined to think that my beliefs are the only "right" ones?
3. Do I trust a higher power, or do I feel I have been abandoned?
4. Am I mad at God for a loss in the past?
5. Do I feel cast out and feel my life is hard and unrelenting?

6. Do I trust that I am safe and connected to a universe that wants to support me?

7. Do I have a ritual that connects me with my God or with nature?

8. Do I long for the magical connection I felt to the universe as a child?

9. Do I have a sense of joy that comes from my purpose in the world?

10. Can I imagine myself connected to everyone and everything?

Our consciousness translates spiritual connection into the language we know. For some of us, the religion we grew up with is the best language; for others, a system of our own choosing makes more sense. Whatever your beliefs or spiritual path, know that the divine will manifest itself in the language and imagery with which you are most comfortable. Daily invite the divine to enter your life through prayer, meditation, or communion with nature. Or, like endurance athletes, connect with the divine through physical exertion.

Be patient as you begin to open your connection. The process requires gentleness, willingness, truth, and, at times, discipline. Honor the connection you currently have and truth will open the door to greater levels of connection.

On all levels, truth heals.

EPILOGUE

If the *truth heals,* why is it so difficult for us to speak the truth? Why have we become a culture so afraid of the truth? Why are we so afraid of the very thing that would set us free to feel better, be healthier, wealthier, calmer, more connected, more supported, and at peace?

The question is worth asking. And the alternative is worth imagining, too.

Imagine a world devoted to truth. Where Nike wins us over with *Truth—Just Do It.* And the Milk Advisory Board inspires our health with *Got Truth?* And politicians wow us with *Random Acts of Truth.* And credit card companies remind us—*Truth. Don't leave home without it.* Imagine a world in which our friends, parents, lovers, spouses, colleagues, and clients love and respect us for telling the truth, and want nothing less than the truth.

Ask yourself these questions:

- How much of my day is really dedicated to the truth?
- How many little, forgettable lies did I tell today?
- How many ways did I gloss over how I really feel in order to save face or not ruffle someone's feathers?

- What would my day, this next hour, this next moment, this next evening, tomorrow morning be like if I really decided to tell the truth?
- What would change?

Put yourself on assignment. See what happens. Let your life and those you love surprise you. You'll surprise them and you might even amaze yourself with how much better you feel and how much easier life becomes day after day. After all, we *can* handle the truth.

Can't you just feel your body exhale? *Aaaaah.* Big sigh of relief. That's how it feels when we tell the truth, ask for the truth, receive the truth, and live the truth. A big sigh of relief, of joy, of gratitude, of satisfaction. There's nothing like it.

It may upset some people for a while when you start to live your truth. But eventually they will see the difference in you, and they'll want the same for themselves. Telling the truth is contagious. We all want it from our elected politicians and from the CEOs heading our corporations, and we would love to see the media tell the truth, but do we have the guts to demand it from ourselves? Demand it from yourself, lay the groundwork for it in your own life, extend it to and allow it from others . . . and your life will transform.

Imagine a world based on truth. Imagine that world for our children and our children's children.

I do.

INDEX

Page references to sidebars are in *italics*.

A

AA (Alcoholics Anonymous), 51,
    114, 126
abandonment, 16, 32, 52, 53, 60,
    89, 173
Abdul, Paula, 25, 26
aboriginal truth practice, 2–3
abuse. *See* specific types of
accidents
    as attention-getting, *30*, 169
    author's experiences with, 64,
        110, 165, 169
    celebrity examples about, 53, 88
    chakras connected with, 31, 35,
        170
    energy system affected by, 7, 17
    patient example about, 31, 33
addictions, 40–41, 42, 51, 59,
        137. *See also* specific types of
aggression, 56, 68, 74, 75–76
AIDS/HIV, 59, 87, 103, 104, 116,
    117, 171, 172

Alcoholics Anonymous (AA), 51,
    114, 126
alcoholism/alcohol abuse
    author's, 6, 46, 51, 91, 110, 112,
        113–114
    celebrity examples about, 19, 20,
        40–41, 42, 53, 59, 66, 79
    chakra connected with, 44
    Mother's, 14
    patient examples about, 51, 73
Alicia, 54–57
Allen, Woody, 67
alternative healing/medicine, 54,
    133–134, 153–154, 164, 169
Alzheimer's disease, 161–162
American Express, 172
Amish forgiveness example,
    101–102
anger
    chakras related to, 80, 88, 93,
        95, 97

M

N

O

P

NOTES

NOTES

HAY HOUSE TITLES
OF RELATED INTEREST

YOU CAN HEAL YOUR LIFE, the movie,
starring Louise L. Hay & Friends
(available as a 1-DVD program and an expanded 2-DVD set)
Watch the trailer at: **www.LouiseHayMovie.com**

THE SHIFT, the movie,
starring Dr. Wayne W. Dyer
(available as a 1-DVD programme and an expanded 2-DVD set)
Watch the trailer at: **www.DyerMovie.com**

***

BE HAPPY, Release the Power of Happiness in YOU, by Robert
Holden PhD

EVERYTHING I'VE EVER DONE THAT WORKED,
by Lesley Garner

***SAVING SAMANTHA, A Young Woman's Escape From
Childhood Hell*** by Samantha Weaver

YOU CAN HAVE WHAT YOU WANT, by Michael Niell

YOU CAN HEAL YOUR LIFE, by Louise L. Hay

***WHY MY MOTHER DIDN'T WANT ME TO BE A PSYCHIC,
The Intelligent Guide to the Sixth Sense*** by Heidi Sawyer

*All of the above are available at your local bookstore,
or may be ordered by contacting Hay House (see next page).*

We hope you enjoyed this Hay House book.
If you would like to receive a free catalogue featuring additional
Hay House books and products, or if you would like information
about the Hay Foundation, please contact:

Hay House UK Ltd
292B Kensal Road • London W10 5BE
Tel: (44) 20 8962 1230; Fax: (44) 20 8962 1239
www.hayhouse.co.uk

***

Published and distributed in the United States of America by:
Hay House, Inc. • PO Box 5100 • Carlsbad, CA 92018-5100
Tel: (1) 760 431 7695 or (1) 800 654 5126;
Fax: (1) 760 431 6948 or (1) 800 650 5115
www.hayhouse.com

***

Published and distributed in Australia by:
Hay House Australia Ltd • 18/36 Ralph Street • Alexandria, NSW 2015
Tel: (61) 2 9669 4299, Fax: (61) 2 9669 4144
www.hayhouse.com.au

***

Published and distributed in the Republic of South Africa by:
Hay House SA (Pty) Ltd • PO Box 990 • Witkoppen 2068
Tel/Fax: (27) 11 467 8904
www.hayhouse.co.za

***

Published and distributed in India by:
Hay House Publishers India • Muskaan Complex • Plot No.3
B-2 • Vasant Kunj • New Delhi - 110 070
Tel: (91) 11 41761620; Fax: (91) 11 41761630
www.hayhouse.co.in

***

Distributed in Canada by:
Raincoast • 9050 Shaughnessy St • Vancouver, BC V6P 6E5
Tel: (1) 604 323 7100
Fax: (1) 604 323 2600

***

Sign up via the Hay House UK website to receive the Hay House
online newsletter and stay informed about what's going on with your
favourite authors. You'll receive bimonthly announcements
about discounts and offers, special events, product highlights,
free excerpts, giveaways, and more!
www.hayhouse.co.uk